LIGHT BULBS, SWITCHES and BATTERIES

HANDS-ON ELECTRICITY
for Young Scientists

LIGHT BULBS, SWITCHES and BATTERIES

HANDS-ON ELECTRICITY
for Young Scientists

Published by
Heron Books, Inc.
20950 SW Rock Creek Road
Sheridan, OR 97378

heronbooks.com

Special thanks to all the teachers and students who
provided feedback instrumental to this edition.

Fourth Edition © 1977, 2021 Heron Books.
All Rights Reserved

ISBN: 978-0-89-739241-9

Any unauthorized copying, translation, duplication or distribution, in whole
or in part, by any means, including electronic copying, storage or transmission,
is a violation of applicable laws.

The Heron Books name and the heron bird symbol are registered trademarks
of Delphi Schools, Inc.

Printed in the USA

13 May 2021

At Heron Books, we think learning should be engaging and fun. It should be hands-on and allow students to move at their own pace.

To facilitate this we have created a learning guide that will help any student progress through this book, chapter by chapter, with confidence and interest.

Get learning guides at
heronbooks.com/learningguides.

For teacher resources,
such as a final exam, email
teacherresources@heronbooks.com.

We would love to hear from you!
Email us at *feedback@heronbooks.com.*

Your YOUNG SCIENTIST JOURNAL

Scientists love to explore the world and how things in it work. They like to go new places and discover things they've never seen before.

They also like to keep track of what they find. They often fill books with notes and drawings of what they see, and include their thoughts and questions about it. These books are called *science journals*.

What's fun about a science journal is that you can use it to draw pictures or sketches of things that interest you. You can write down ideas you have about things, make maps, write down questions you have and things you want to find out more about. You might even stick in it samples of things you find—flowers, bugs, leaves, feathers, spider's webs—who knows what?

The learning guide that goes with this book will sometimes ask you to look at things and make notes or drawings in a journal of your own.

Whatever you put in your science journal, it will be full of your own personal discoveries. No two journals are alike.

You can use a journal like the one shown here, or you can use a notebook of your choice. You might even want to make your own science journal and use that.

Whichever type of journal you choose, it will be a place to keep drawings and notes about what you are finding out about the world and how it works.

So get ahold of a science journal, or make one, and then get going to see what you can find out. Who knows what might be waiting for you?

IN THIS BOOK

1 WHAT MAKES THINGS MOVE? — 1
    Doing Work — 2
    Energy — 4

2 DIFFERENT KINDS OF ENERGY — 7
    Heat Energy — 8
    Light Energy — 10
    Motion Energy — 11
    Electrical Energy — 12
    Energy Moves Things — 13

3 STORED ENERGY — 15

4 ENERGY CHANGES — 19
    Changing Where the Energy Is — 20
    Changing the Kind of Energy — 21
    Storing Energy — 22
    Something to Know About Energy — 23

5 INSIDE ATOMS — 27
    Very, Very Small — 27
    Very, Very, Very Small — 28
    Conductors — 30
    Insulators — 31

6 LIGHT BULBS — 33

7	**BATTERIES**	37
	Stored Energy	37
	Terminals	40
8	**CIRCUITS**	43
	Short Circuit	44
	Making a Circuit	46
9	**SWITCHES**	49
	Using a Switch	53
10	**VOLTAGE**	55
	Different Voltages	57
	Changing the Voltage	58
11	**RESISTANCE**	61
	Changing the Resistance	65
12	**CURRENT**	67
13	**A LAW ABOUT ELECTRICITY**	73
	Ohm's Law	75
	Ohm's Law Experiment #1	
	More Resistance Makes Less Current	81
	Ohm's Law Experiment #2	
	More Voltage Makes More Current	82
	Ohm's Law Experiment #3	
	Using Ohm's Law to Run a Motor	83
14	**LOOKING AHEAD**	85

1

Light bulbs, switches and batteries all have something to do with electricity. And electricity is a special kind of energy.

So before we start talking about light bulbs, switches, batteries and electricity, it makes sense to talk about energy first.

DOING WORK

The world is full of things that move. Some of them, like the wind, animals and ocean waves, move on their own.

Others move because humans have created ways to make them move. Engines move cars down the road. They move boats across the sea and planes through the air.

And many things made by people have parts that move. Think about bicycles, pencil sharpeners, toasters and clocks. Bicycles have wheels that go around, pencil sharpeners have handles and blades that turn, toasters have parts that move toast up and down. Clocks have hands that go around.

In science, when you make something move, it's called "doing work." That's right, **doing work** means moving something. It's that simple.

Cars, boats and planes do work by moving people. So do bicycles. Pencil sharpeners do work by moving blades that shave a pencil into a sharp point. Clocks move their hands around and measure time. These all do work because they move things.

Now let's think for a minute about electricity.

    Does it do work?

    Does it move things? Sure!

An electric car or an electric train moves people from one place to another. An electric fan moves air to cool you off. An electric saw moves a spinning blade to cut through pieces of wood.

Anything that causes something to move is doing work.

ENERGY

For something to move, it needs energy.

Cars, boats, trains and planes use energy to move things. Their energy usually comes from gasoline, which burns in an engine and makes wheels or propellers or jets move.

You need energy to ride your bicycle. You get this energy from food. When you run out of energy, your bike stops moving, unless you're coasting down a long hill!

An electric fan needs energy to do its work. Where does it get it? You plug the fan into a wall outlet and turn it on. Electricity makes the blades go around, they move the air, and this cools you off.

You can't hold energy in your hand. You can't smell it or taste it. Why? Because **energy** is simply the power to move things. It's the power to do work.

What makes things move?

Energy!

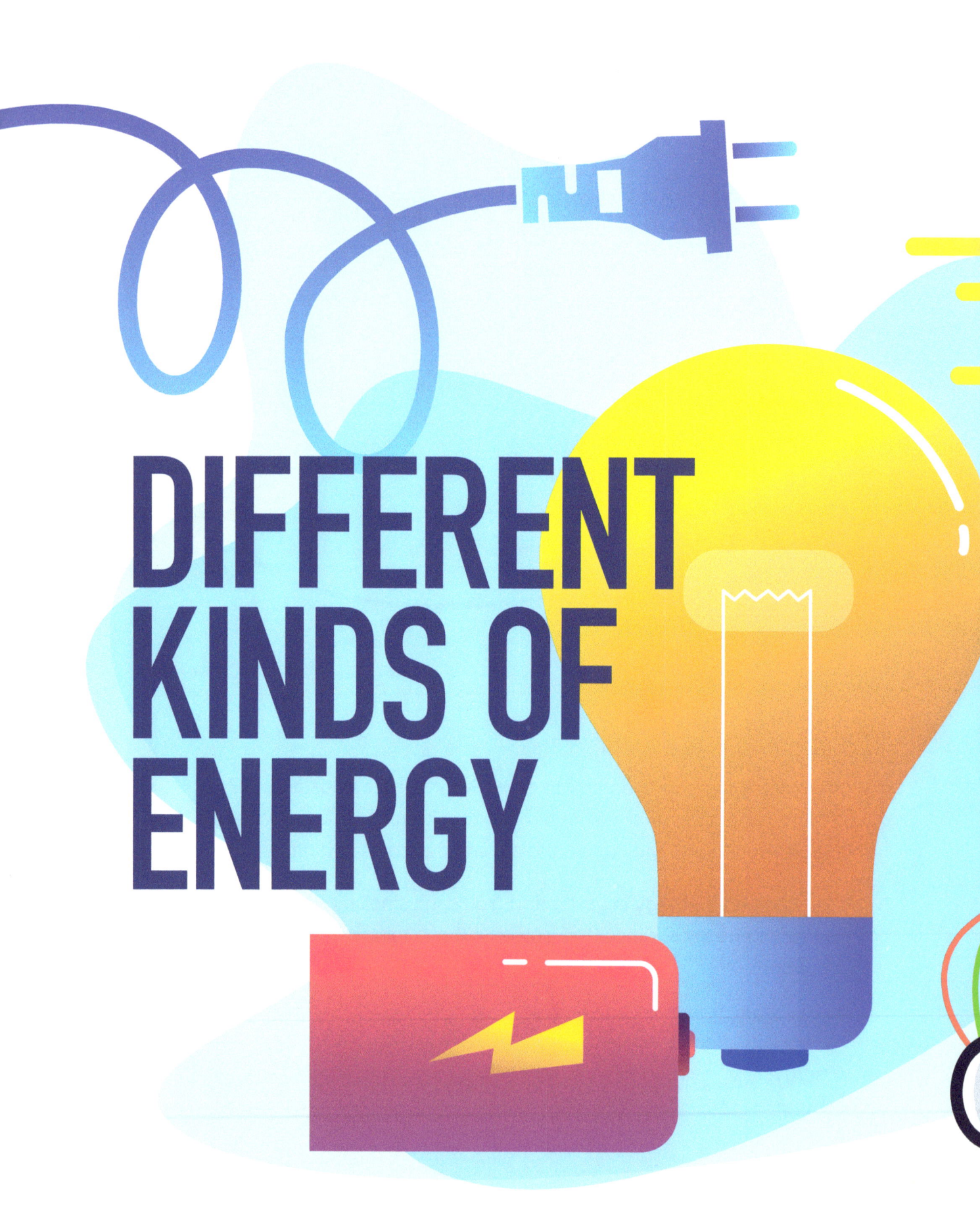

2

There are many different kinds of energy, and we use them all to move things.

HEAT ENERGY

Let's take a look at heat energy.

The sun gives off lots of this sort of energy. You can feel it on warm days. A cooking stove gives off heat energy. So does burning wood.

When you feel heat coming from something that is doing work, what you feel is **heat energy**.

Heat energy can move things. You may, however, not be able to see the things it is moving because they are so small.

Let's take a look at how this works.

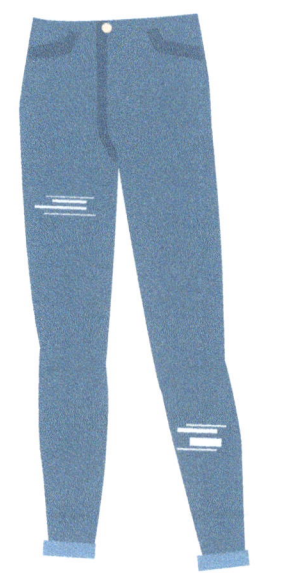

The things around you (chairs, tables, pencils, books, food, cars, planes, clothes) are all made of tiny, tiny parts called **atoms** (AT umz). Atoms are so small you can't see them.

The interesting thing about these tiny atoms is that they are always moving, even though you can't see them doing this. If you touch a wall, you won't feel anything moving. But every little part of that wall is made of trillions and trillions and trillions of tiny atoms. And each atom is moving. It's just kind of jiggling around. The thing about heat energy is that it makes atoms move or jiggle faster. The atoms in a warm wall are jiggling faster than the ones in a cold wall.

If something feels hot, you know its atoms are moving very fast. If they are moving very, very fast, your finger might even get burned. When something feels cold, you know its atoms are moving more slowly. If something is too cold, it can also hurt your finger.

Here's an example of heat energy making something move. If you hold a pan over a fire, its heat energy hits the pan making the atoms of the pan jiggle faster. The faster they go, the warmer the pan gets. You can't see this happening, but you can feel it.

If you then put water in the pan, the water will also start to heat up. Pretty soon not only are the water atoms jiggling, but you can see the water moving too. If you hold the pan there long enough, the water will boil!

LIGHT ENERGY

The sun, stars, candles, light bulbs and burning things give off heat energy along with another kind of energy called **light energy**.

Can light energy make things move? Yes!

Have you ever walked barefoot on a sandy beach on a very hot day? The light from the sun makes the atoms in the sand move faster so the sand feels hot!

A more interesting example might be a solar-powered car. **Solar** (SO lur) means from the sun. A solar-powered car runs from the light energy of the sun. Every year, teams of college students compete to make the best cars that run on the sun's light energy!

MOTION ENERGY

Moving things have energy. They can make other things move by pushing them. This is called the energy of motion or **motion energy**.

Moving air or wind has motion energy. Wind can push a sailboat across a pond, lake or even an ocean!

Moving water has motion energy. The water coming out of a hose can push things in its way. Some people clean things off the sidewalk by spraying water from a hose. In earlier times, people that lived near flowing water used it to move large stones to grind wheat into flour for making bread.

When you push a door closed or move something across a table, you are using motion energy. Anything that is moving has energy. Think about that!

ELECTRICAL ENERGY

Another kind of energy makes things like washing machines, computers and TVs work. Each of these has a wire that plugs into the wall. When you turn one of them on, you start tiny parts of atoms, called electrons (uh LEK tronz), moving through the wire. These moving electrons have energy. This is called **electrical energy** or **electricity**.

Electrical energy from moving electrons is what makes toasters get hot. It's what makes lights shine and computers run.

Besides an outlet on the wall, another way to get electrical energy, or electricity, is from a battery. Batteries put out electrical energy that can be used to make things run.

ENERGY MOVES THINGS

All these different kinds of energy move things.

Heat energy from a stove will make atoms move faster so you can fry an egg in a pan.

Light energy from the sun can make a solar-powered car go down the road.

Motion energy can kick a soccer ball into a goal.

And the electrical energy from a battery can make a toy car race across a room.

3

When you **store** something, you put it away until you need it. For example, you might buy a whole bunch of pencils and pens, then store them away until you need them.

Stored energy is energy that is being kept somewhere and isn't doing work right now. It *could* do work but it isn't yet. It is being saved up to move things later on.

If you hook a rubber band around your finger and pull the rubber band back, it will fly off when you let it go. Where does it get the energy to fly off? The rubber band picks up energy and stores it as you pull it back. When you let it go, the stored energy makes it fly across the room.

We call the energy in the pulled-back rubber band stored energy. It isn't doing work right then, but it will when you let it go!

A jack-in-the-box is a toy with a spring inside. When you close the jack-in-the-box lid, it pushes the spring down. Energy moves from you to the spring, where it is now stored energy.

When you open the box, the spring can move, and it uses its stored energy to make the clown jump up.

When you pull a wagon up a hill, you are using energy. You could say that the energy is stored in the wagon. If you let go of the wagon, it will roll back down the hill. You could use the stored energy to get a ride!

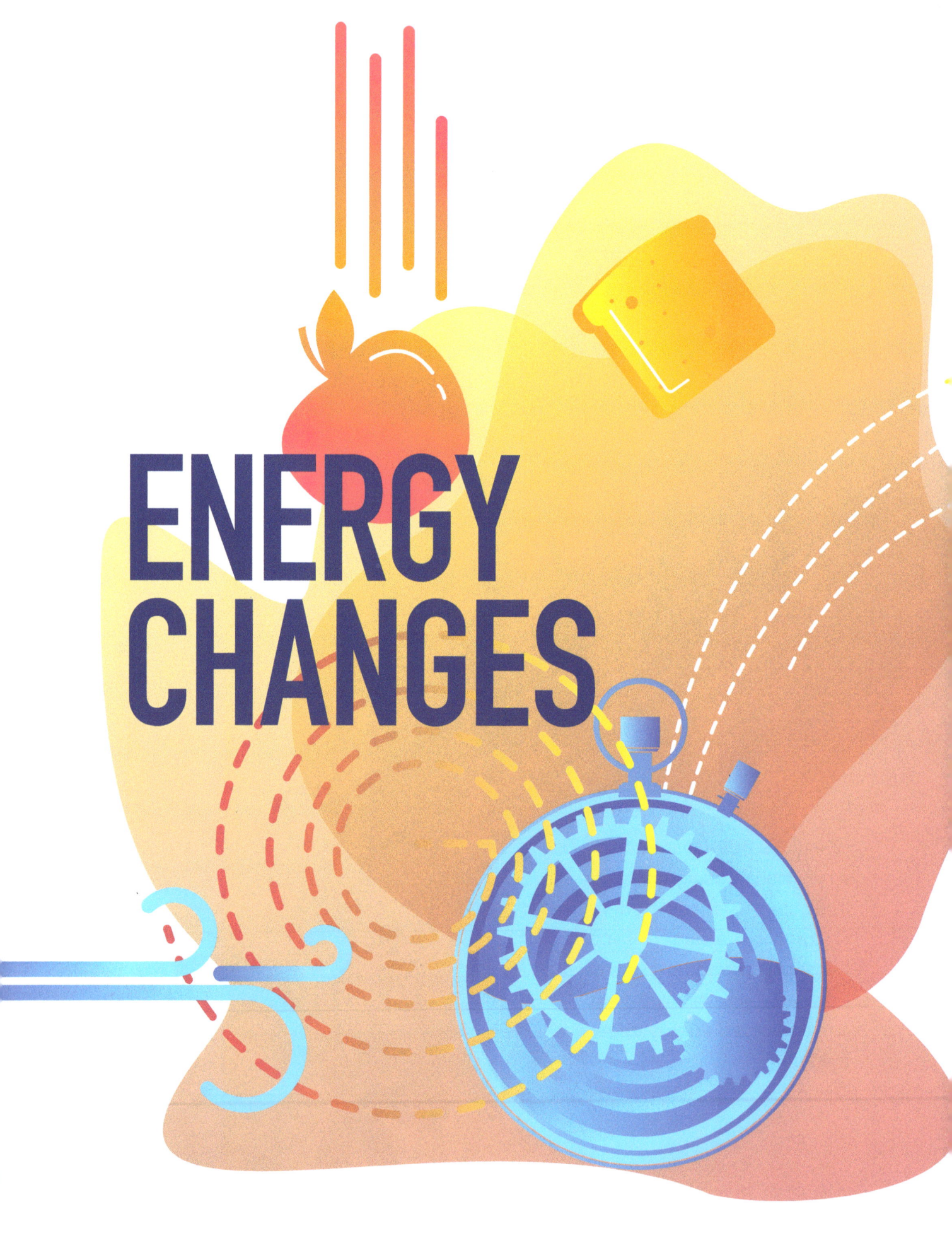

4

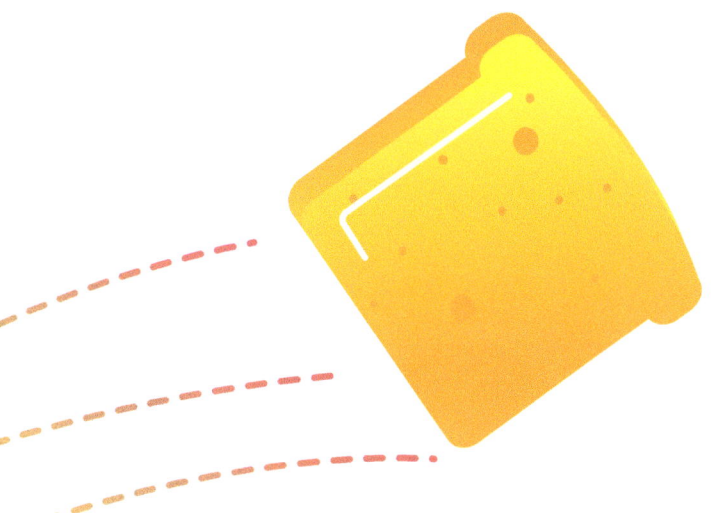

Energy moves things all the time. The wind blows, kids ride scooters and bikes, people ski, machines dig holes and fix roads, trains run and computers work. But amazingly, all this energy doesn't get used up or lost, it just gets changed in some way.

How does this happen? There are three main ways.

1. The energy moves from one object to another. That's a change.

2. The energy changes from one kind of energy to another. For example, it might change from electrical energy to heat energy, or from motion energy to electrical energy.

3. The energy becomes stored energy to be used later.

Let's talk about each one of these.

CHANGING WHERE THE ENERGY IS

First, let's look at energy moving from one object to another.

A push is one way of moving energy from one thing to another. Let's say you use the motion energy of your foot to kick a ball.

The energy goes from your moving foot to the ball.

Now the ball has energy. It's moving! If it hit someone who wasn't looking, it could knock them over.

Here's another example.

A girl swings a bat and hits a ball. The energy moves from the motion of the girl to the motion of the bat. When the bat meets the ball, its energy then moves to the ball.

CHANGING THE KIND OF ENERGY

Now, let's look at energy changing to a different kind of energy.

An example of this is a light bulb.

Inside a light bulb is a wire. When electrical energy passes through the wire, it gets hot and begins to glow. Some of the electrical energy in the wire has changed to heat and light energy.

The same kind of thing happens in a toaster.

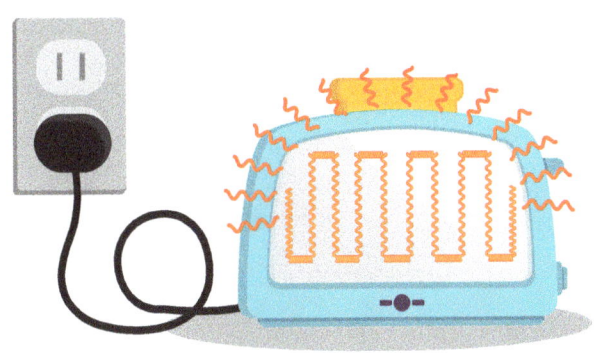

Electrical energy flows through a wire to the toaster and along the wires inside the toaster. The wires get red-hot. The electrical energy in the wires changes to heat energy. It's the heat energy that toasts the bread.

There are many ways that one kind of energy can change to a different kind. This happens all the time.

For example, motion energy can change to heat energy. Try rubbing your hands together hard and fast. Can you feel them getting warmer? When you did this, the motion energy of your hands changed to the heat energy you feel.

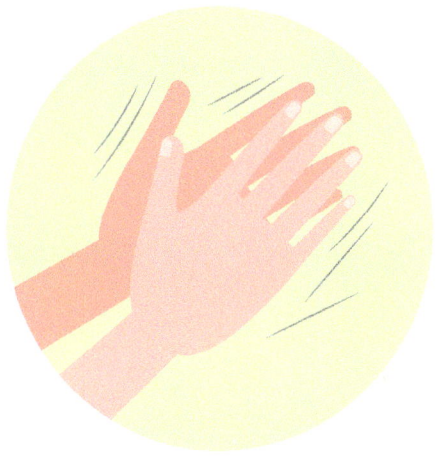

STORING ENERGY

Another way you can change energy is to store it. This is a way to save it up so it can be used later.

You store energy when you grow vegetables in your garden. As plants grow, they store energy from the sun. When you eat them, your body takes the stored energy and turns it into energy you can use to run, jump and do all sorts of things.

Instead of running on batteries, some clocks run on energy from a spring inside. You turn a knob to wind up the clock and this stores energy. Here's how. Turning the knob twists the spring inside the clock tight. The motion energy from your hand goes through the knob and gets stored in the spring. As the spring slowly unwinds, it lets the stored energy out bit by bit and moves the hands of the clock.

SOMETHING TO KNOW ABOUT ENERGY

There is a law about energy that is useful to know. But first we must understand what kind of law we're talking about.

One type of law is the kind that people make, agree on, and try to follow. A simple example is the law that says all drivers must stop at stop signs. This law helps people move around safely in cars. In some places there are laws about putting money in a parking meter, or keeping dogs on leashes. There are laws against stealing and laws that prevent people from harming others. These are all laws that people agree are useful.

Another kind of law is called a **natural law** or a **scientific law.** This type of law describes the particular way that something will *always* act in nature (the physical world).

For example, if you drop something it will *always* fall toward the earth.

It is *always* true that the harder you push or throw something, the faster it will go.

Water will *always* freeze below a certain temperature.

There is a natural or scientific law about energy. It has been observed and is always true that energy never gets used up or lost. It either moves from one object to another, changes to a different kind of energy, or is stored.

But the amount of energy remains the same.

When you kick a soccer ball, it may seem like some energy has been all used up. It's true that you used some of your energy. But the energy is not gone. It has just moved from your leg into the soccer ball moving across the field.

This is called the **law of conservation of energy.**

Conservation (kon sur VAY shun) is keeping things, rather than losing them. The law of conservation of energy says that when energy is used to move things, it is always conserved, it always remains and is never lost. It just changes in some way.

If you think about it, this is a fascinating law!

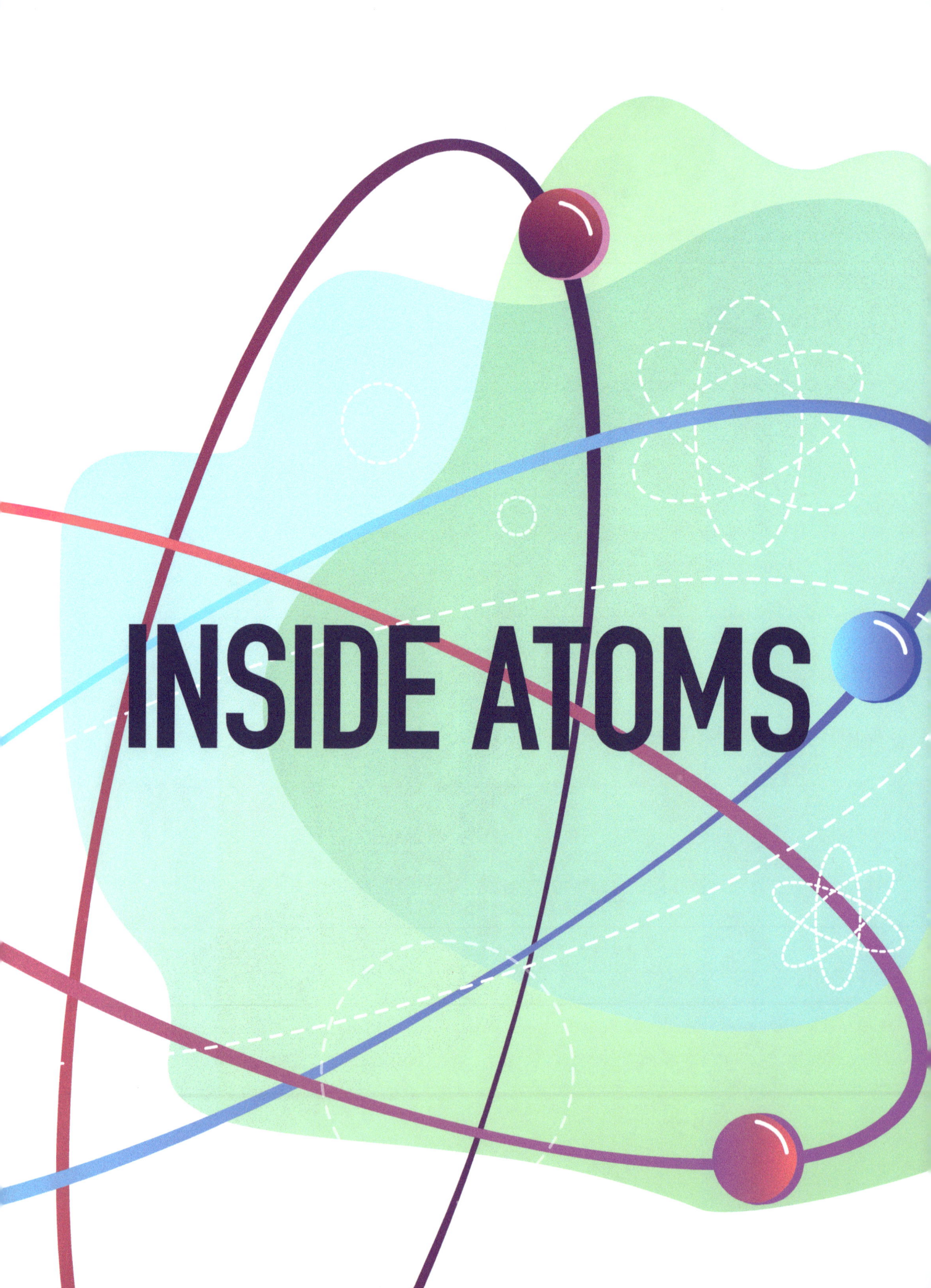

5

VERY, VERY SMALL

As we talked about earlier, all objects are made of very tiny pieces called atoms. Atoms are so small that we cannot see them. It takes many, many atoms together to make something that is big enough to see.

If you looked at a brick house from far away, you wouldn't see the individual bricks. They are too small to see from far away. If you were closer, you could see the bricks.

This explains why you can't see atoms. They are too small. In fact, atoms are so small you can't even see them with most microscopes. The kind of microscopes used to look at atoms cost millions of dollars!

All objects are made of atoms.
A pencil is made of atoms.
Paper is made of atoms.
Water and air are made of atoms.

The period at the end of this sentence is *millions* of atoms in size.

VERY, VERY, VERY SMALL

If atoms are very, very small, the things inside an atom must be very, very, VERY small!

And they are.

Here's a drawing that shows what the three parts of an atom are.

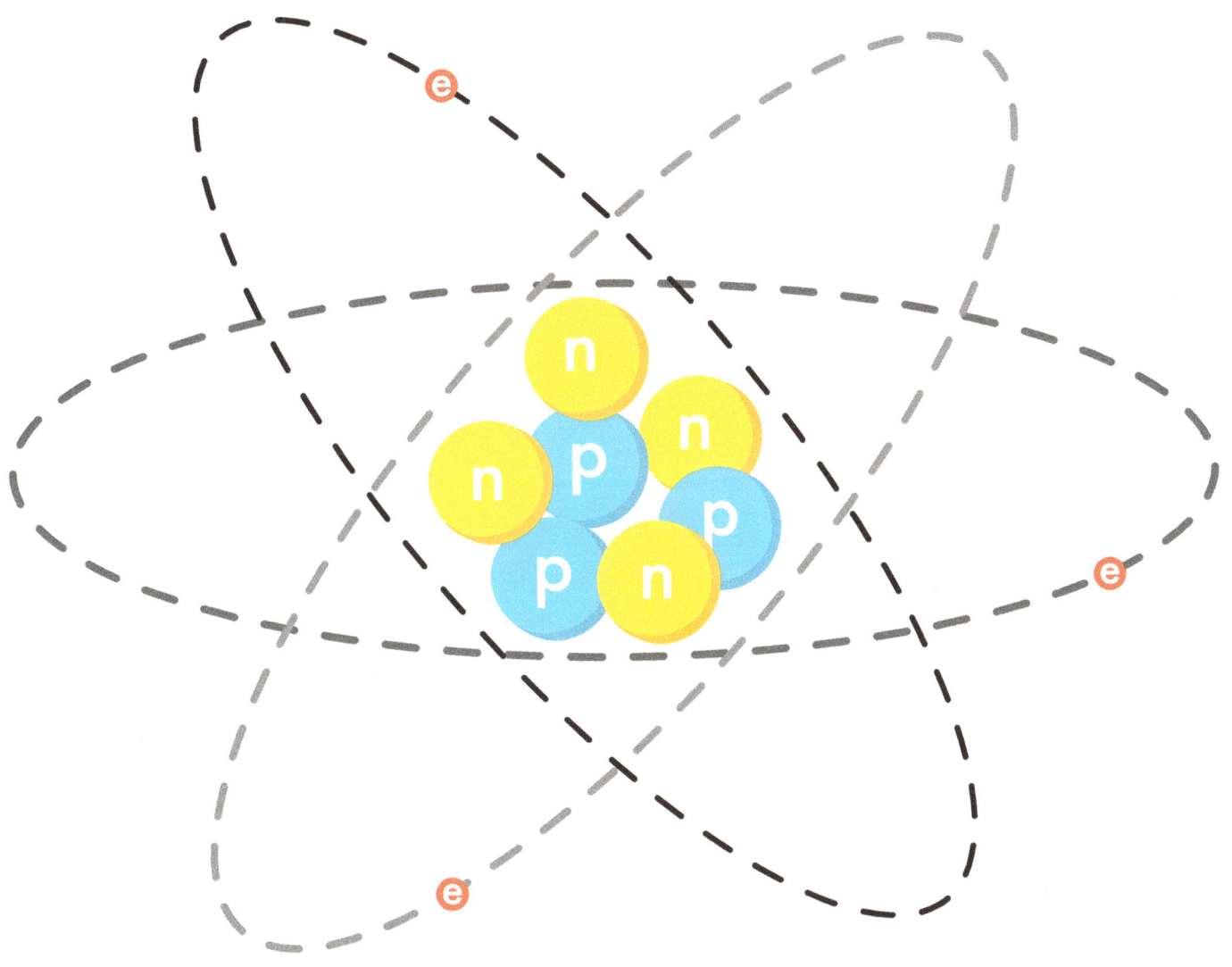

Protons and **neutrons** are the parts that are grouped together in the middle of the atom.

Electrons are the lightest and smallest part of atoms and they move around the other parts.

Different objects have different kinds of atoms. Some types of atoms have many protons, neutrons and electrons, while others have only a few. But even though atoms of different substances are different, all things are made of atoms, and all atoms have these three parts.

CONDUCTORS

Atoms try to hold on to their electrons, but sometimes they get away. In copper and silver and other metals, some electrons can get away from their atoms easily. They move to atoms nearby.

In electricity, the word **conduct** (kun DUKT) means to let electrons move between atoms. When electrons can move easily between the atoms of a material, it's called a **conductor** (kun DUKT ur).

Copper and silver are conductors. Many metals are conductors. This means they let electrons move easily between the atoms.

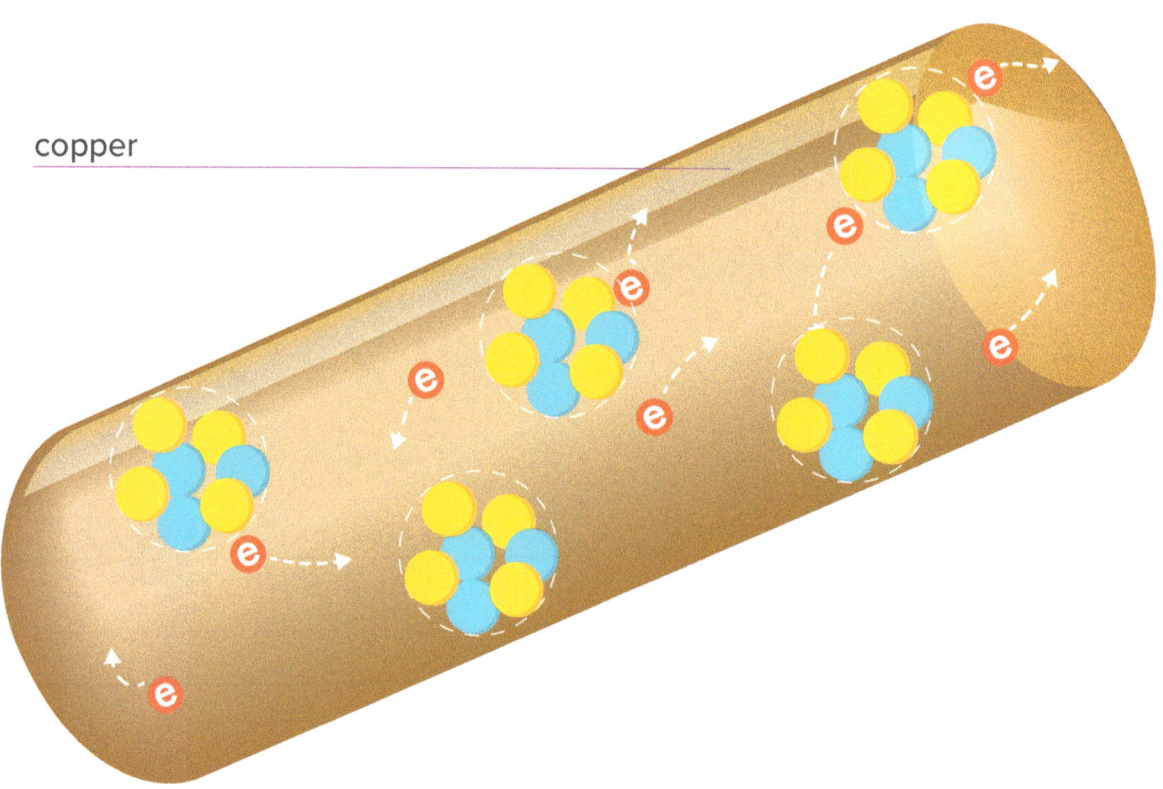

copper

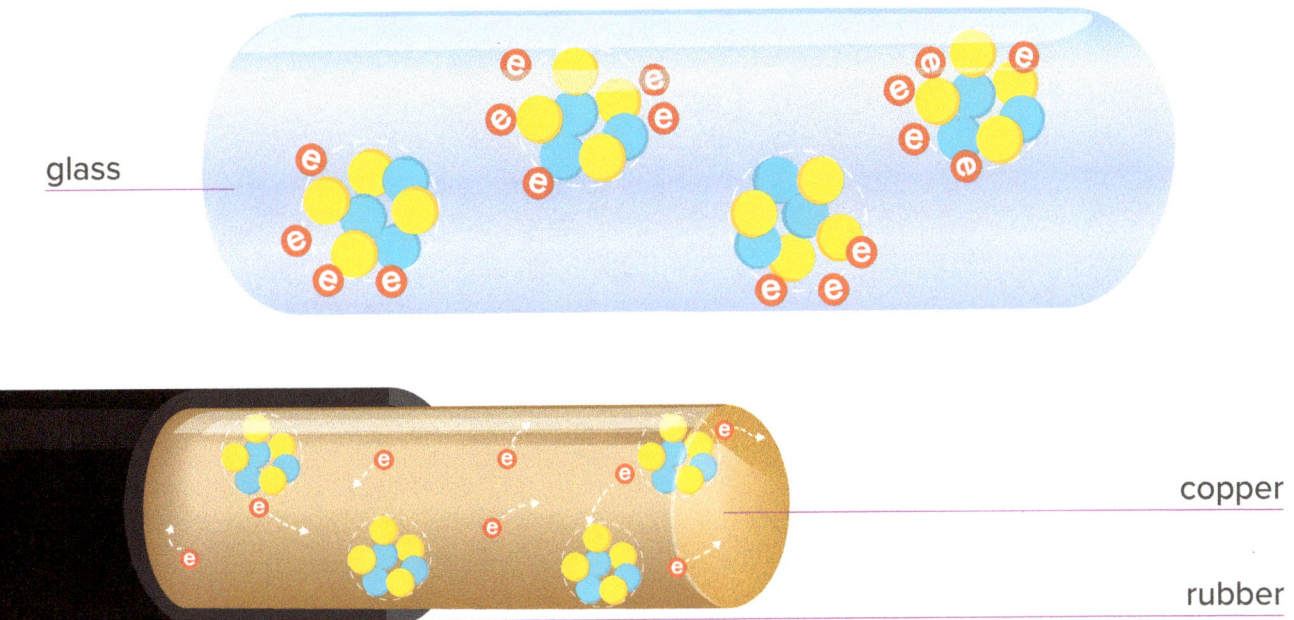

glass

copper

rubber

INSULATORS

When we talk about electricity, **insulate** (IN suh late) means to keep electrons from moving through. **Insulators** (IN suh lay turz) are materials like glass, wood and plastic. The electrons are stuck much tighter to the atoms and can't move between them easily.

An electrical wire that is made of a good conductor like copper will usually have a good insulator like plastic or rubber on the outside. This way the electrons will move down the wire easily while the insulator keeps them from getting outside it.

Some materials are not very good conductors or insulators. They let electrons move some, but not a lot. An example is a pencil lead.

We call something a *conductor* if it is a very good conductor. Silver and copper are conductors.

We call it an *insulator* if it is a very good insulator. Rubber and plastic are insulators.

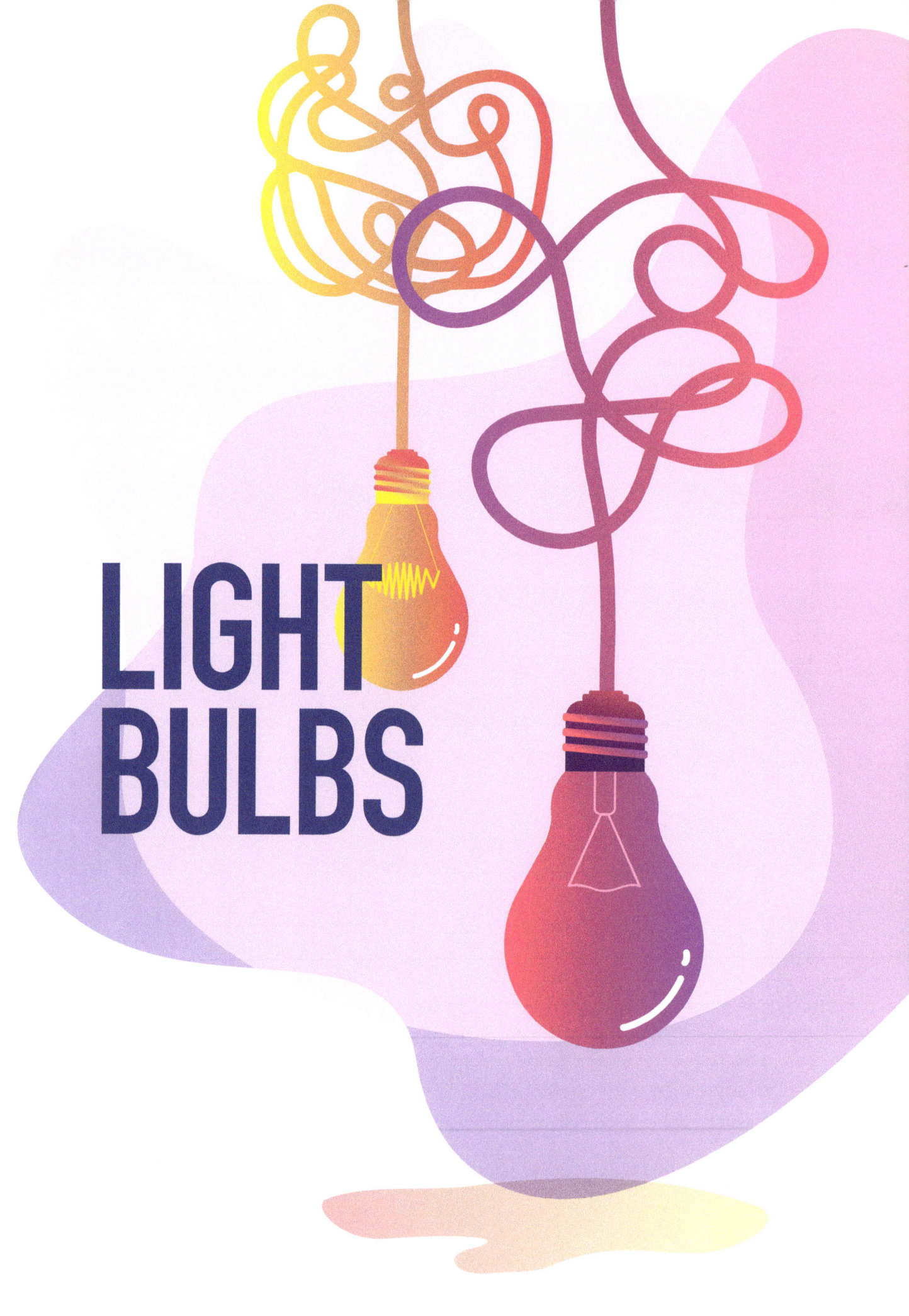

Light bulbs are very handy. We use them every day. Take a look around you and see how many light bulbs are in a single room. Imagine how many light bulbs there are shining all around the world, providing light for people to see when otherwise it would be dark.

Let's explore a light bulb and discover just what is happening with the atoms and electrons that produces this miraculous effect.

When a light bulb shines, it is because electrons are moving through it. Here is how one kind of light bulb works.

It has glass on the outside and metal wires on the inside. One of these wires is made of a special metal and is very thin. This is called the **filament** (FIL uh munt). The wires that connect to the filament are very good conductors, but the metal in the filament is not.

When you turn a light bulb on, you let electrons start moving along the wires and through the filament. Moving along the wires is easy because the wires are such good conductors.

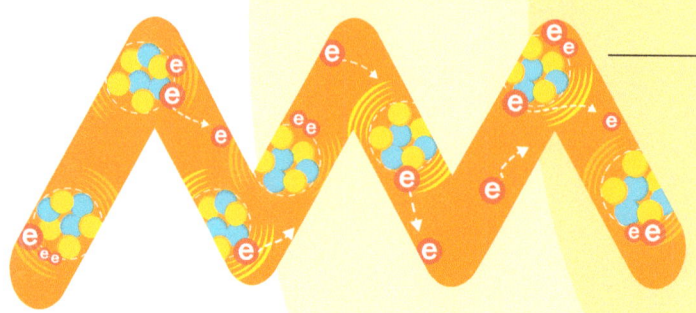

But when the electrons get to the thin filament, they stop moving so easily because the filament is not a good conductor. Its atoms try to hold on to the electrons and keep them from moving along.

The moving electrons hit the atoms of the filament. Sometimes they bounce off and sometimes they stick. They bounce into one another and all of the atoms in the filament start moving faster.

With the electrons bouncing into the atoms and the atoms bouncing into each other, all this motion energy is changed to heat energy and the filament gets very hot. It gets so hot that it starts to turn fiery red. Then it gets even hotter, and glows white. The glowing white filament gives off light.

This all happens so fast that you usually can't even see the red. The light bulb looks like it turns white and gives off light instantly.

The **socket** of a light bulb is what the bulb sits in. When you screw a light bulb into a socket, the conductors on the light bulb connect to conductors in the socket. The socket is connected to wires that bring electrons into the bulb. When they hit the filament, the electrons create a lot of heat energy and the filament gets so hot that it shines.

Not all light bulbs look like this one, but all light bulbs change electrical energy into light energy and heat energy.

Just think, before the light bulb came along in the late 1800s, people had to burn things to create light when it was dark. From candles to oil lamps, from lights that burned gas to fireplaces burning logs, light energy came from energy stored in wax, oil, gas or wood.

Now the electrical energy we are so used to is easily changed to light energy by the millions and millions of light bulbs in the world!

7

STORED ENERGY

A **battery** is something you can put energy in to store it. It is a container full of stored energy.

When you want to use that energy, you connect the battery to something. It then gives its energy by making electrons move. It uses up its stored energy slowly, giving you electricity over a long period of time.

If we connect a battery to a light bulb with wire, the battery will push electrons through the wire to make the filament in the light bulb give light.

You might think the electrons are racing through the wire very quickly, but actually each electron only moves a very small amount.

Really! Let's see how that works.

Each atom that makes up the wire has lots of electrons, so the wire is crowded with millions and millions of electrons!

There are so many electrons that the battery can only push some into the first bit of the wire. These electrons push other electrons along so that they all move forward just a bit. It's kind of like people crowding onto a full bus.

The electrons in the light bulb's filament get moved along too. This heats up the filament so much it glows.

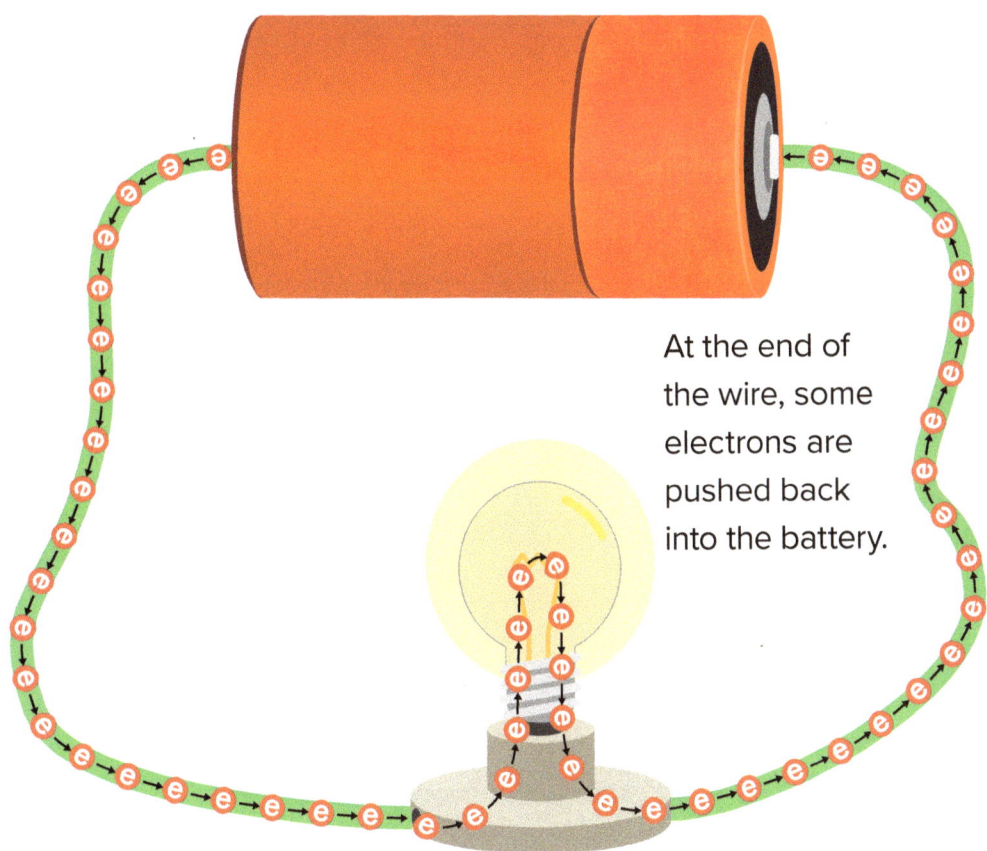

At the end of the wire, some electrons are pushed back into the battery.

Imagine a hose full of water. If you push a little bit of water in one end, it pushes the water forward and some water comes out the other end. It is the water that was already near the end of the hose that comes out.

Electrons work the same way.

The wire connects the battery to the light bulb. It's like a hose for the electrons to travel in. The stored energy of the battery makes the electrons move. The moving electrons in the light bulb make it shine.

TERMINALS

On a battery, there are two places to connect wires, called **terminals** (TUR muh nulz).

One terminal is called the **minus terminal**, and it usually shows a – (minus) sign. This is where the electrons come out of the battery.

The other terminal is called the **plus terminal**, and it usually shows a + (plus) sign. This is where electrons come back into the battery.

Here's how it works.

A battery has a certain amount of stored energy. When it is hooked up, it pushes electrons out the minus terminal. It also lets them in at the plus terminal.

When the stored energy in the battery is used up, it can't push any more electrons out or let any more in. Then we say the battery is "run down" or "dead." It doesn't work anymore because it doesn't have any more stored electrons that can move easily.

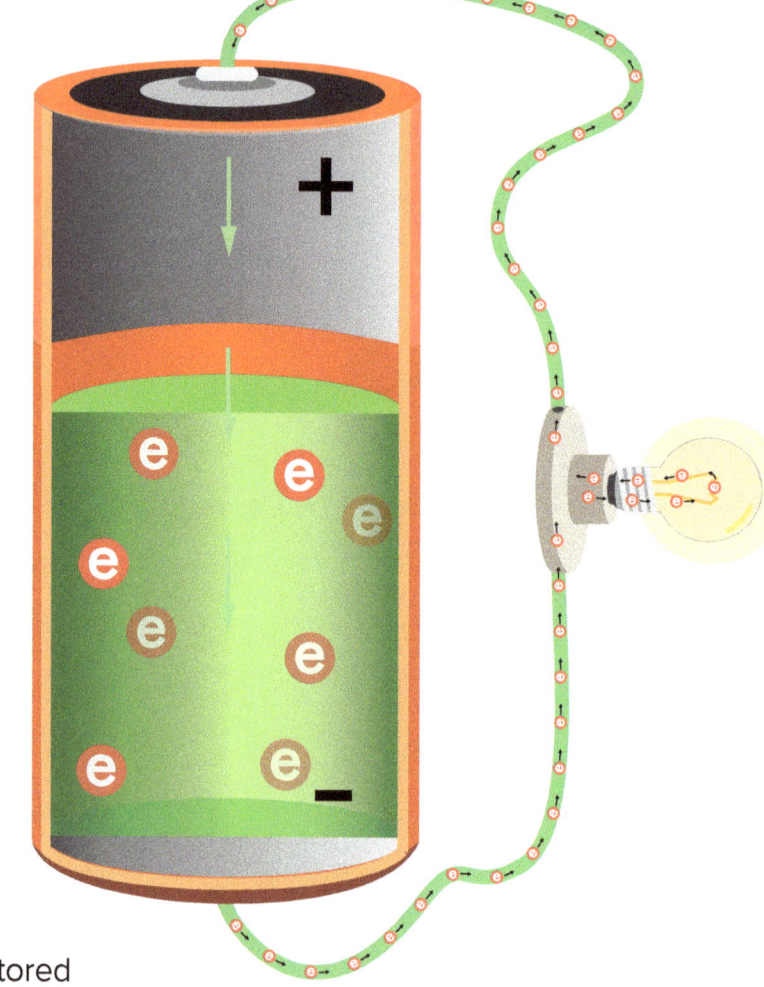

The first battery ever made was by a man named Alessandro Volta over 200 years ago.

Fig. 283. — Pile de Volta.

Nowadays, batteries can be small enough to fit into a watch and large enough to store energy for a whole village.

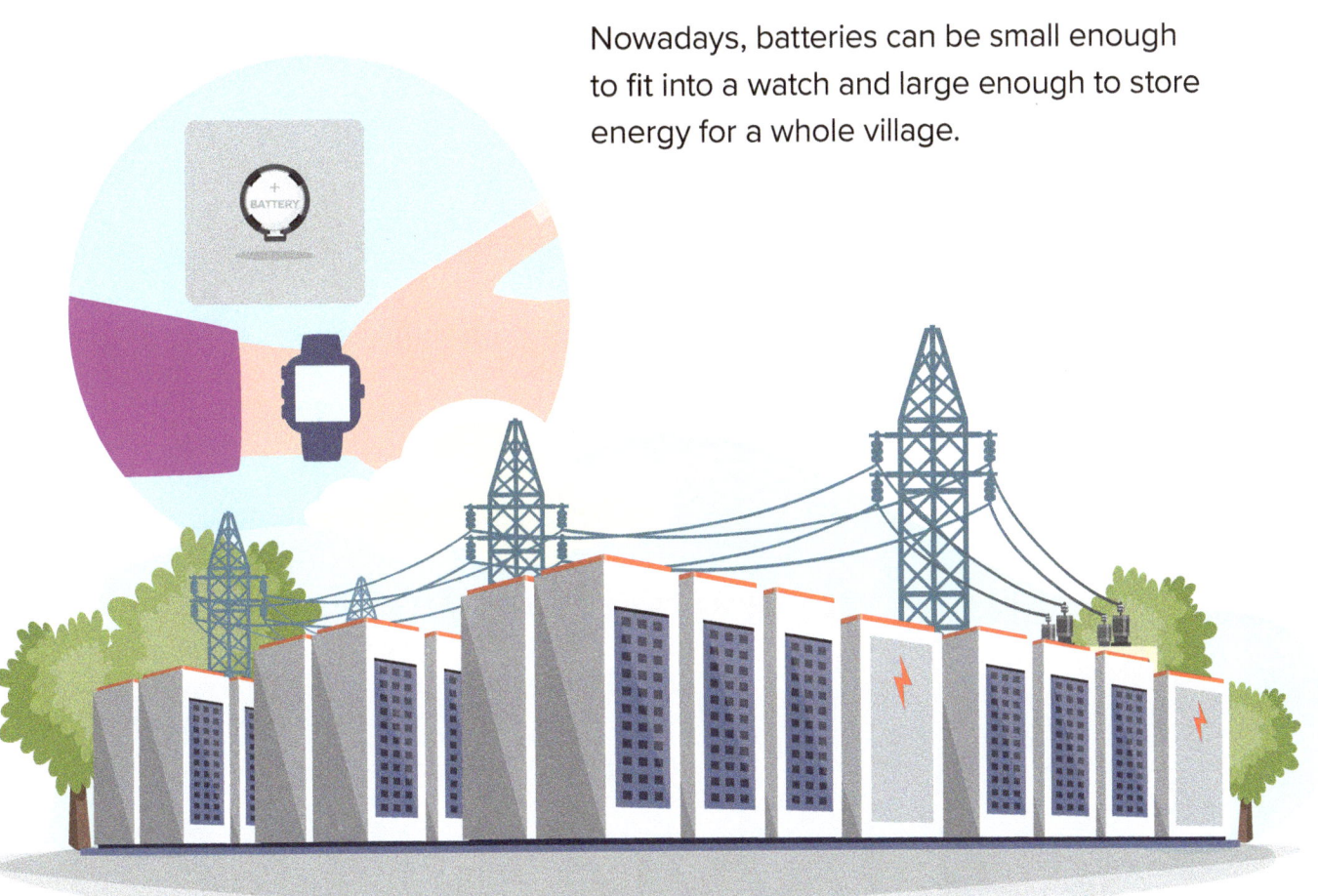

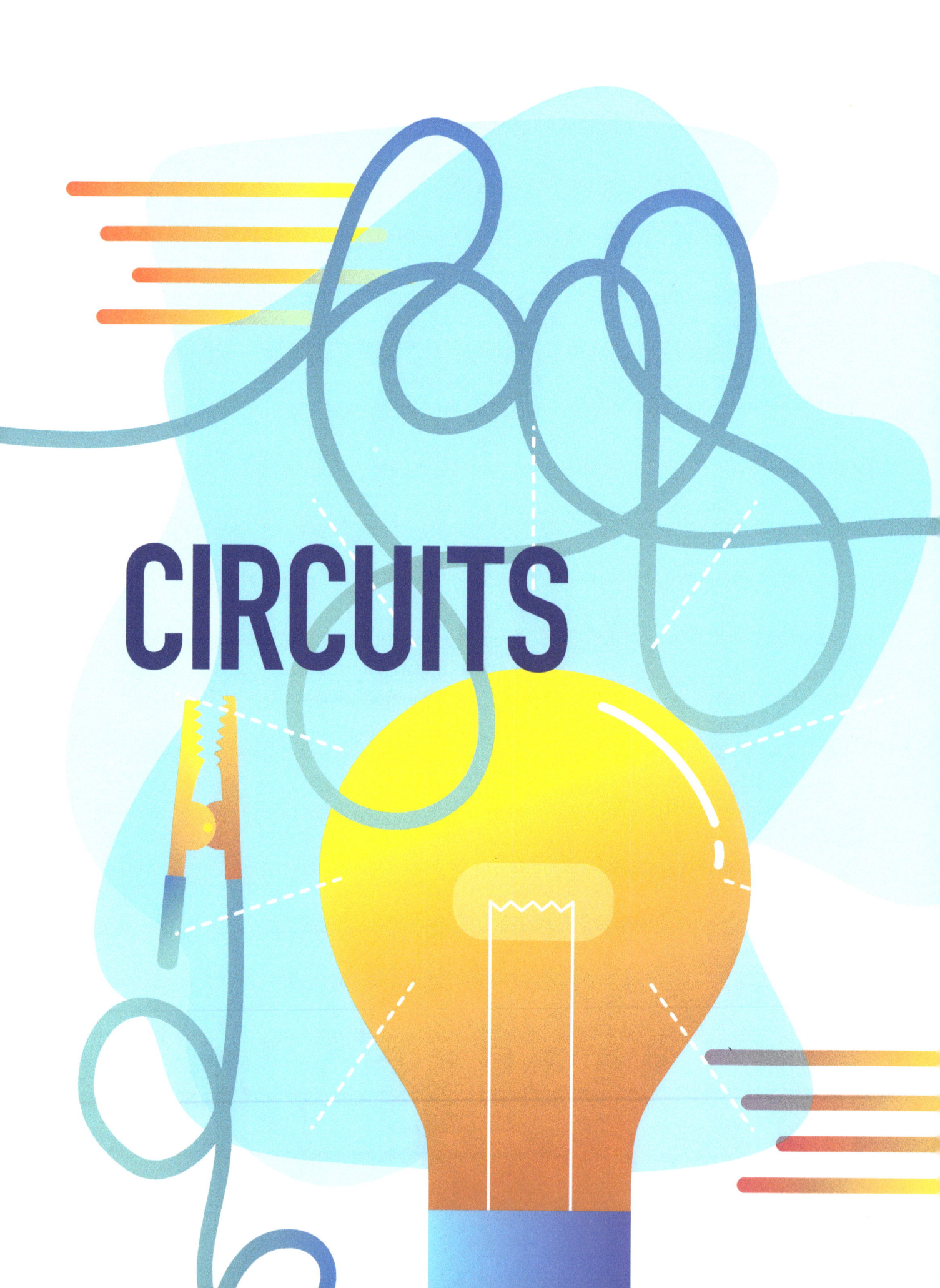

8

When a battery and a light bulb are connected, electrons move in a circle. They go from the battery to the light bulb and back to the battery. This is called a **circuit** (SUR kit). A circuit is a path that electrons travel on, in this case from the battery through the wires and light bulb, then back to the battery. It is a whole loop that goes around and ends up back where it started.

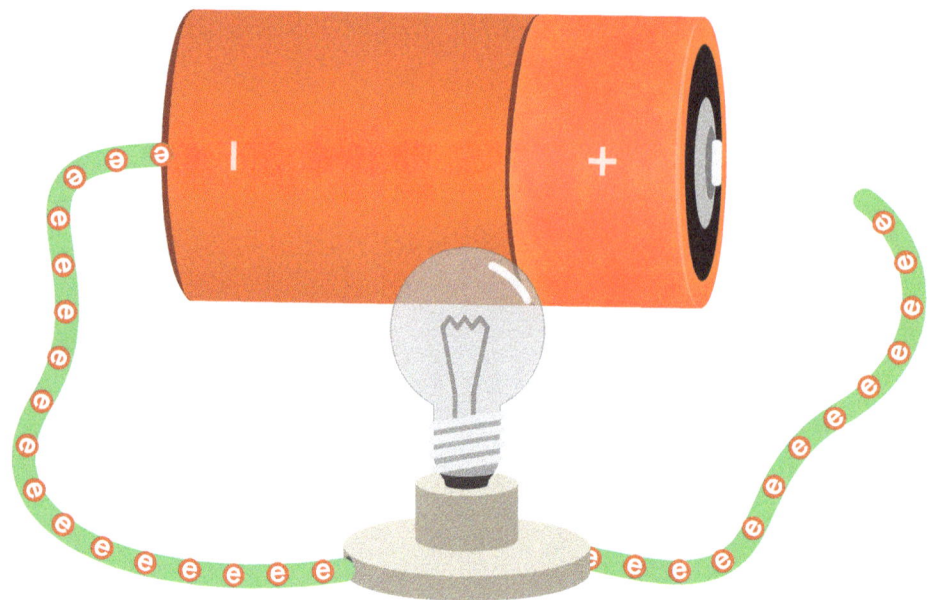

If you unhooked the wire from the battery, or cut it, this would break the circuit. The electrons wouldn't flow.

When the light bulb shines, you know you have a complete circuit!

SHORT CIRCUIT

What do you think would happen if you connected one terminal of a battery to the other terminal without a light bulb in the middle?

What would happen is that the electrons would flow. You would have a circuit.

But the energy stored in the battery would get used up very fast. Why would this happen?

A battery has a certain amount of stored energy. In a circuit with a light bulb shining, the energy has some work to do because the filament is not a good conductor. The atoms in the filament slow down the electrons.

If there is no light bulb to slow down the electrons, they move *too* easily. A battery can push so many electrons into a wire so fast that even a good conductor wire might get hot. It might even melt! The battery will run out of energy pretty fast.

This kind of circuit is what we call a **short circuit**. It could be called an "easy circuit," because the electrons move too easily. But it's just called a short circuit or a "short."

When you are building circuits, you want to avoid making short circuits because they can get so hot.

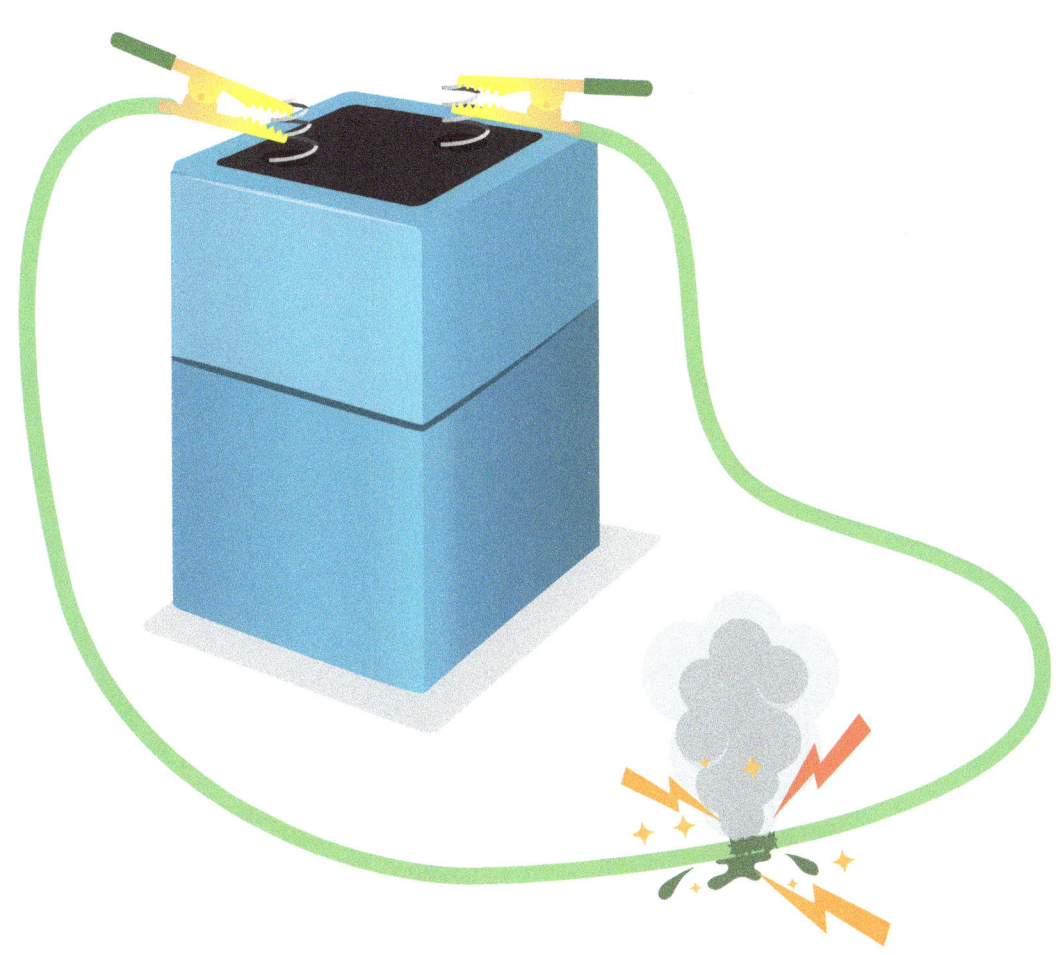

MAKING A CIRCUIT

For this activity you will need

- 2 alligator clip wires
- 1 6-volt mini light bulb
- 1 bulb socket
- 1.5-volt (1 ½ volt) D-cell battery
- 1 battery holder

Steps

① Attach a piece of wire from a battery to an empty light bulb socket. Attach another piece of wire to the other side of the socket that goes back to the battery. Be sure that the clips are attached to the metal parts of the battery and sockets.

② Put a bulb in the socket and see how the battery makes the bulb shine.

③ Take off one wire so the light isn't shining.

④ In your science journal, explain what's happening with the electrons when you make a circuit. Explain what happens when you disconnect the circuit.

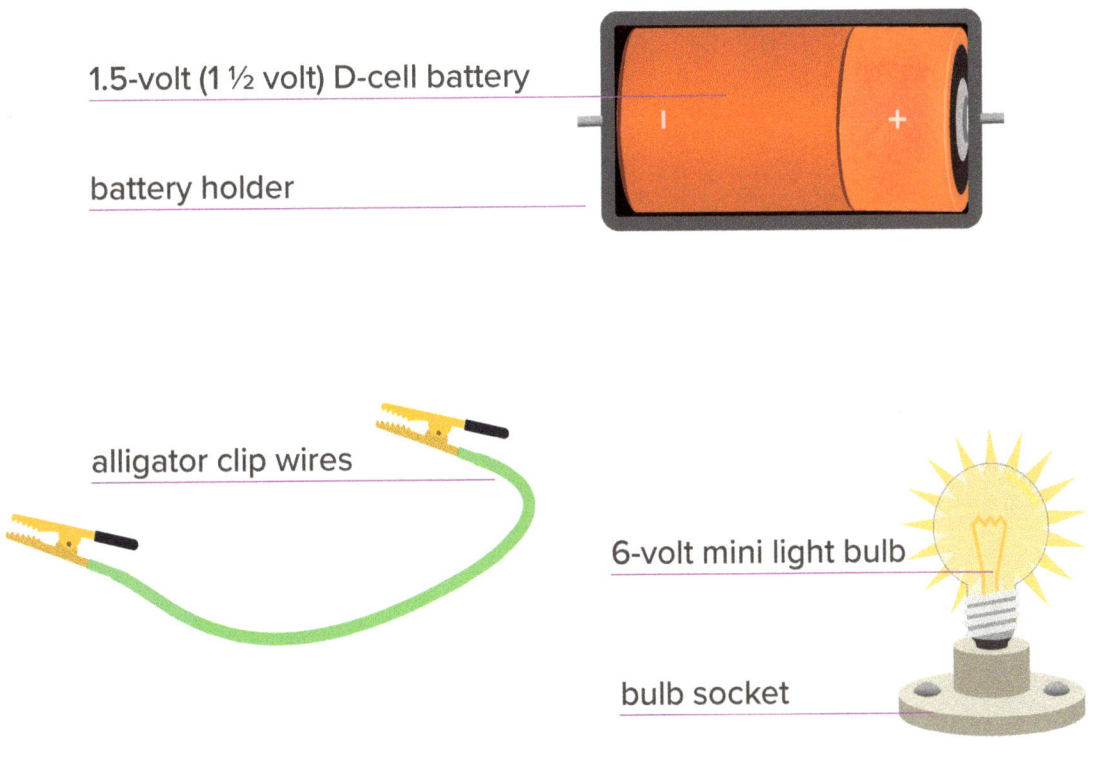

1.5-volt (1 ½ volt) D-cell battery

battery holder

alligator clip wires

6-volt mini light bulb

bulb socket

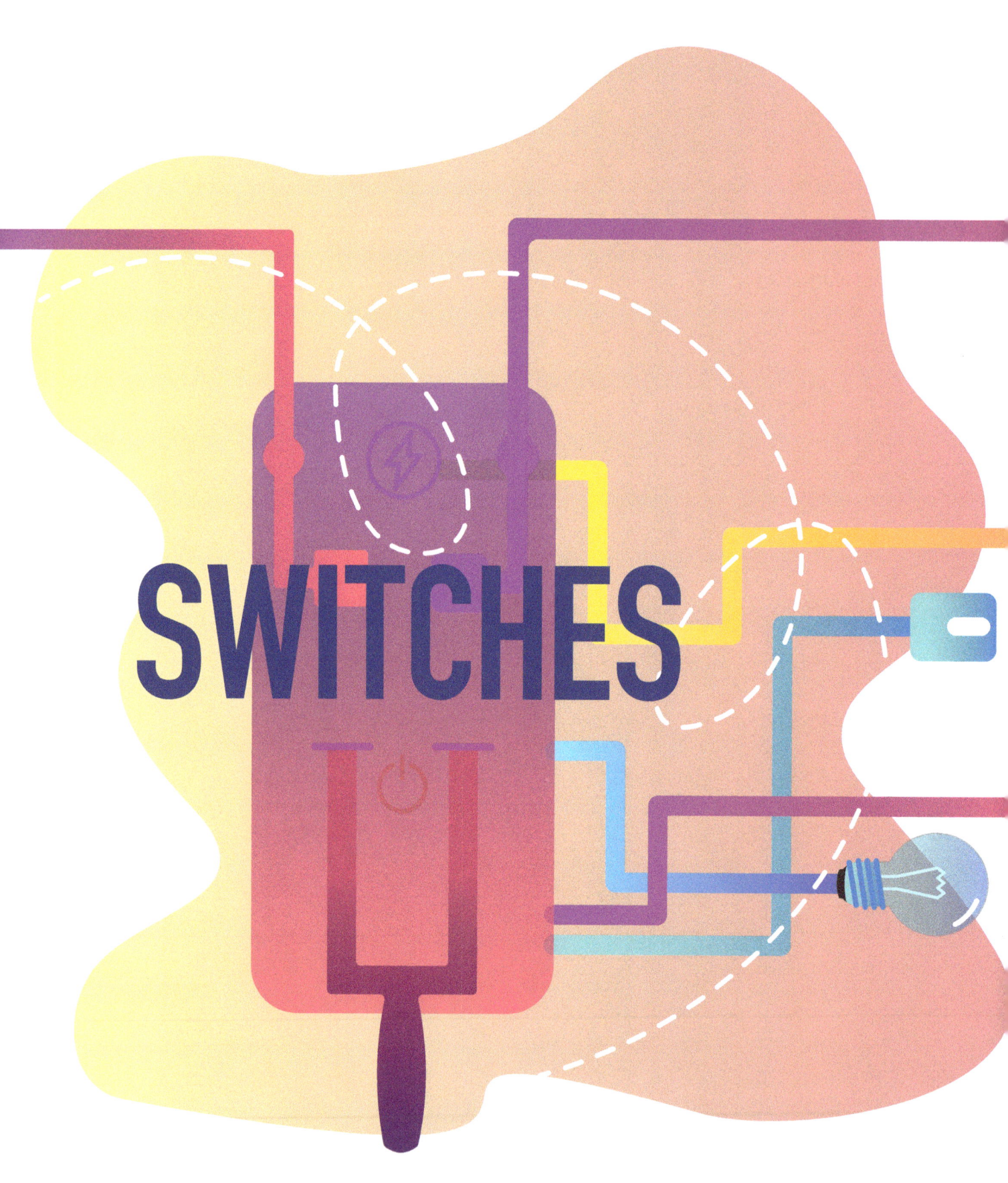

9

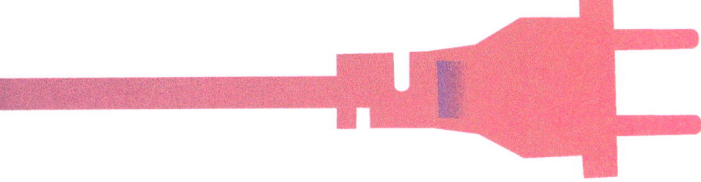

A **switch** is something you use to turn electricity on and off. Switches are used to start and stop the electrons that are moving in a circuit.

You now know that unless it is part of a circuit, a light bulb won't shine.

If there is a gap in a circuit, the electrons won't be able to move across the gap. Air is a pretty good insulator. It doesn't let electrons flow through it.

But if you connected the wires across the gap, electrons could flow.

Suppose we connect the wires with a piece of metal.

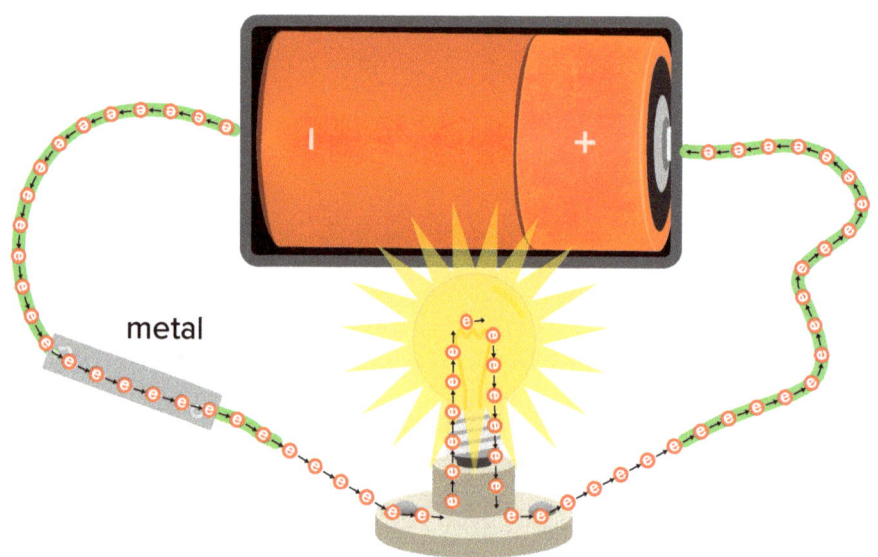

As long as the piece of metal is there, the electrons can move all the way around the circuit and the light will be on.

What if we move the metal so it doesn't connect the wires?

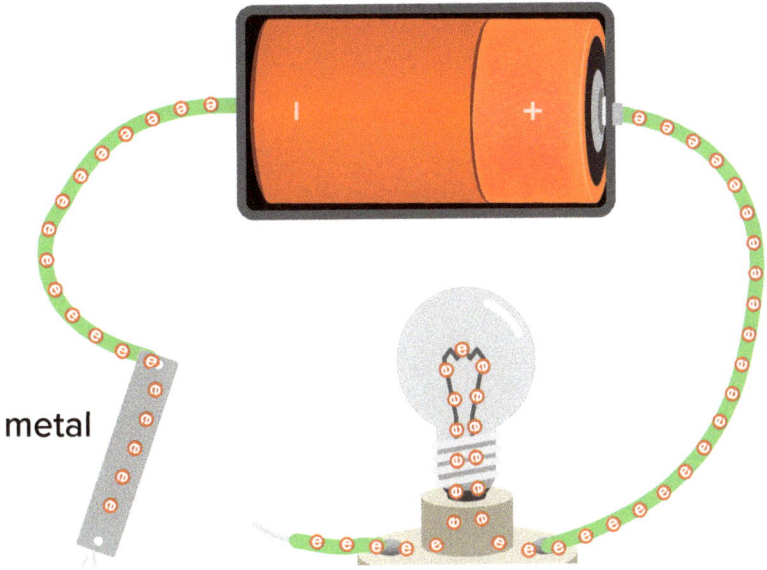

Now the electrons can't move through the circuit. The light bulb is off.

An **electrical switch** is something that can let electrons move, or can stop them from moving along. If you move it one way, the electrons go along. If you move it another way, the electrons stop.

This type of electrical switch is called a **knife switch**, because the metal part looks a bit like a knife.

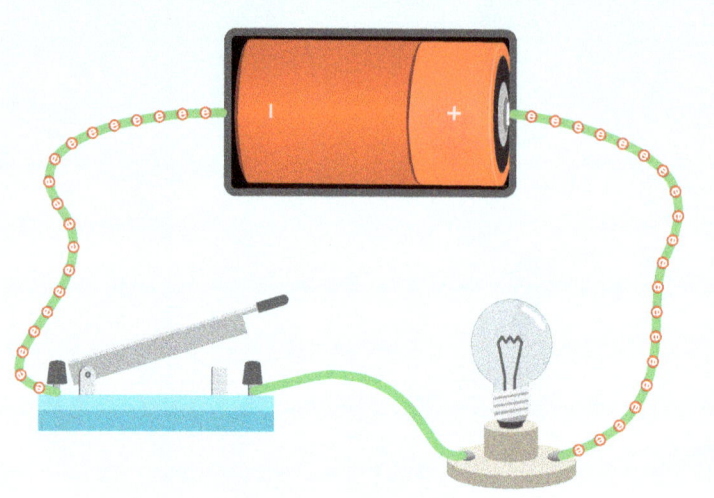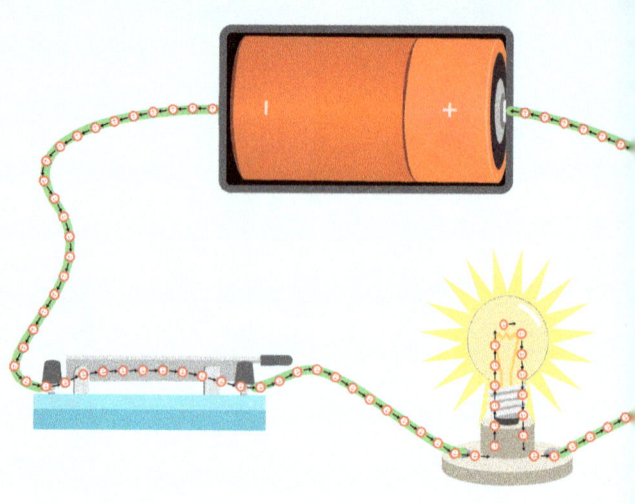

This is where the switch comes in! When a switch like this is open, the electrons can't flow and the light won't shine.

When a switch like this is closed, it completes the circuit. The electrons can move and the light shines.

Light bulbs, toasters, ovens, vacuum cleaners, televisions and computers all have switches. Although they don't look like knife switches, they work the same way. When you turn them on, they complete the circuit and let the electrons move along. When you turn them off, the circuit is broken and the electrons stop moving.

There are many different kinds of electrical switches. Some are round. Some are hidden in the wall. For some you pull a string.

Whatever they look like, they all do the same thing. Switches let electrons move along or they stop them from moving.

USING A SWITCH

For this activity you will need

- 3 alligator clip wires
- 1 6-volt mini light bulb
- 1 mini bulb socket
- 1 knife switch
- 1 1.5-volt (1 ½ volt) D-cell battery
- 1 battery holder

Steps

1. Make a circuit with a battery, socket, light bulb and wires.

2. Next, add a switch to your circuit.

3. Open and close the switch and see what happens to the light.

4. In your science journal, draw or explain what's happening with the electrons when you open and close the switch.

5. Take everything apart and put it away. Or just open the switch to turn the light off. You will use your circuit later.

10

Some kinds of batteries push electrons harder than other kinds of batteries do. For example, cars have batteries in them. Car batteries push electrons harder than the kind of battery you are using for the activities in this book.

Scientists use a word to describe how hard a battery pushes electrons. It's called **voltage** (VOHL tij). A car battery has a higher voltage than, for example, a flashlight battery.

We can see how this works using water and hoses for comparison. With water, we don't call it voltage, we call it pressure.

There is a big difference between the water coming out of a garden hose connected to a normal faucet and the water coming from a fire hose connected to a fire hydrant!

The fire hydrant pushes water much harder. The water pressure is much higher.

With batteries and electricity, when electrons are pushed harder, we say there is a higher voltage.

DIFFERENT VOLTAGES

People make batteries with different voltages.

Voltage is measured by volts. A **volt** is just a certain amount of push from a battery. Two volts push harder than just one volt. Four volts push even harder than two.

Remember the name of the man that made the very first battery? His name was Alessandro Volta. Because he made the first battery, volts and voltage were named after him!

Most smaller batteries have just 1.5 (1 ½) volts.

Batteries for walkie-talkies and smoke detectors have 9 volts.

Lantern batteries have 6 volts. These are used for camping lanterns or large flashlights.

If you needed 6 volts, you could put four 1 ½-volt batteries together. In fact, inside some 6-volt batteries are four 1 ½-volt batteries.

The size of the battery does not tell you its voltage, which is usually written on the outside of the battery.

But higher-voltage batteries can be quite a bit larger than the batteries used to power smaller electrical devices. For example, a regular car battery is about 12 volts and weighs about 40 pounds. A 500-volt battery that powers an electric car can weigh over 1,000 pounds!

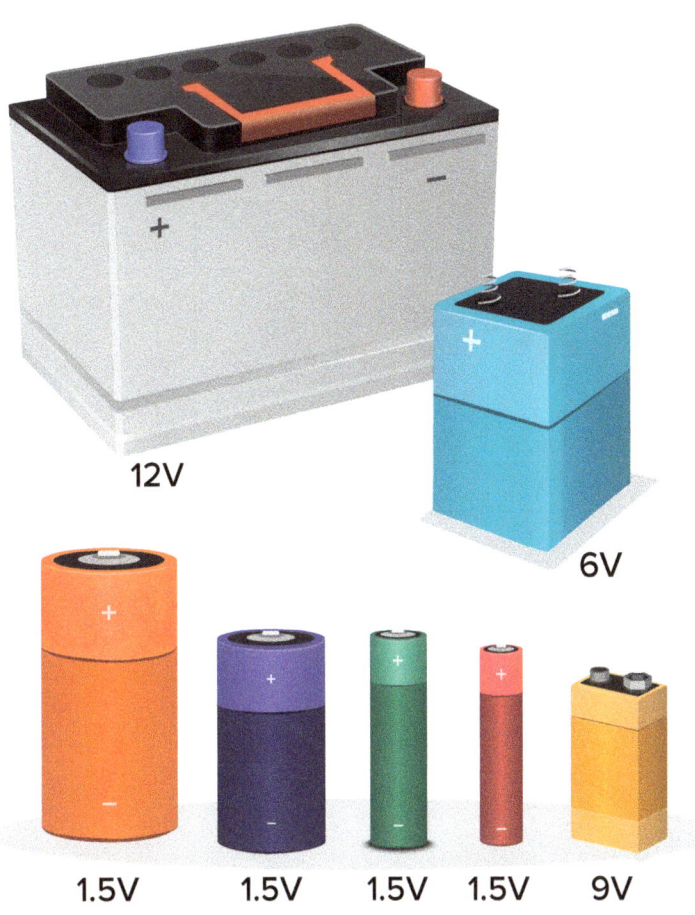

CHANGING THE VOLTAGE

For this activity you will need

- 6 alligator clip wires
- 1 6-volt mini bulb
- 1 mini bulb socket
- 1 knife switch
- 1 6-volt lantern battery
- 4 1.5-volt (1 ½ volt) D-cell batteries
- 4 D-cell battery holders

Steps

1. Make a circuit with wires, a socket and bulb, a switch and a 6-volt battery. Notice how bright the bulb is.

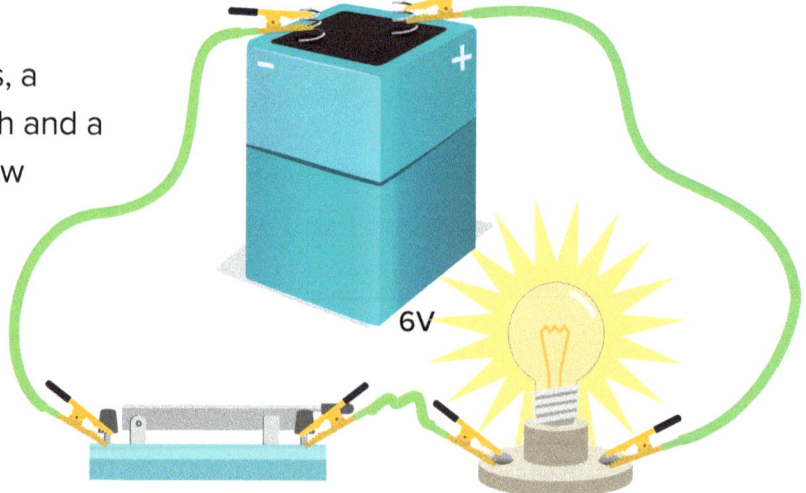

58

② Replace the 6-volt battery with one 1.5-volt battery. See if the bulb lights and, if it does, how bright it is.

③ Add another 1.5-volt battery to make 3 volts. (Remember the electrons flow out from the minus terminal and into the plus terminal. So, be sure to attach the minus terminal [-] of one battery to the plus terminal [+] of the other.) See if the bulb lights and, if it does, how bright it is.

④ Add another 1.5-volt battery to make 4½ volts. Notice how bright the bulb is.

⑤ Use four 1.5-volt batteries together to make 6 volts. Notice how bright the bulb is. Is it as bright as with your original 6-volt battery?

⑥ In your science journal, explain how changing the voltage affected the brightness of the bulb.

11

As you know, electrons do not always just race along. It depends on what kind of material they are in.

In conductors like metal, the electrons move easily.

In insulators like plastic, the electrons don't move easily. The atoms do a better job of hanging on to them.

In a light bulb filament, which is part conductor and part insulator, the electrons bounce around quite a bit while atoms try to hold onto them.

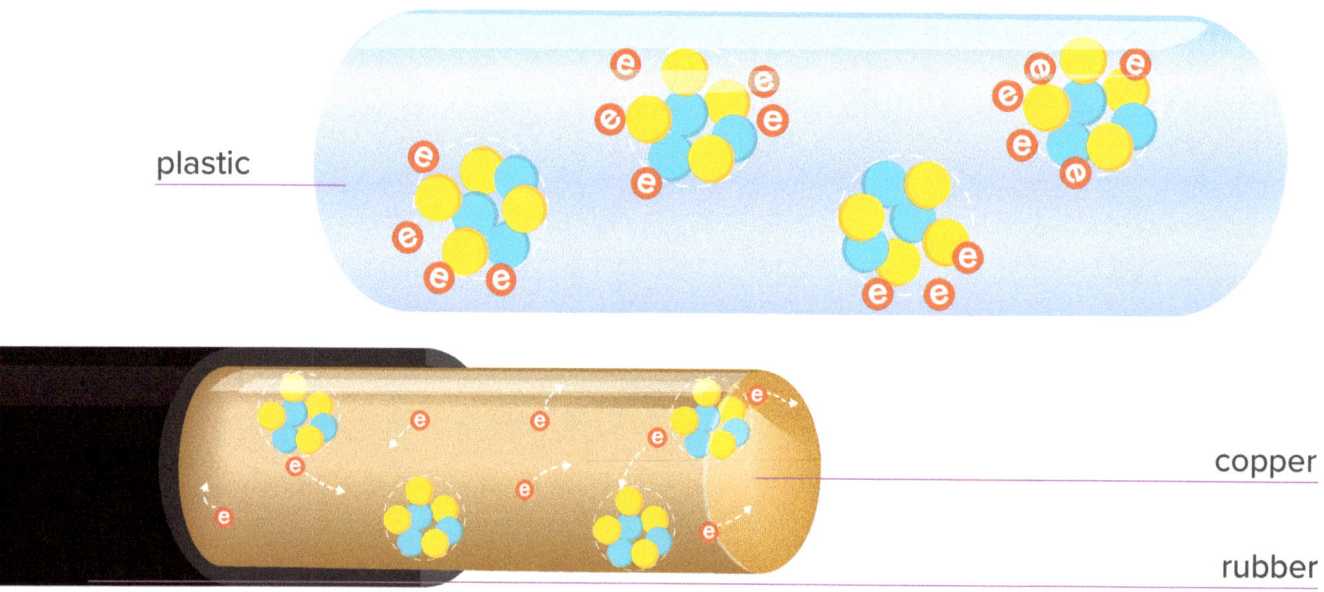

plastic

copper

rubber

When you fight against something or try to stop it, we say you **resist** it. In a circuit, you could say the atoms fight against the easy movement of electrons. They resist the flow of electrons.

Some kinds of atoms resist more, and some don't resist so much. The atoms in insulators resist a lot and the atoms in conductors hardly resist at all.

The bouncing and holding on to electrons by atoms is called **resistance** (ri ZIS tunts).

Wires have only a little resistance. Filaments in light bulbs have quite a bit of resistance, but not as much as plastic or rubber. In the filament, the resistance doesn't stop the flow but causes more bouncing of electrons.

A circuit with a bright bulb has resistance, but mainly in the filament, which gets hot and bright.

If you added another light bulb, the resistance would increase. Not as many electrons would move and the light bulbs would shine less brightly.

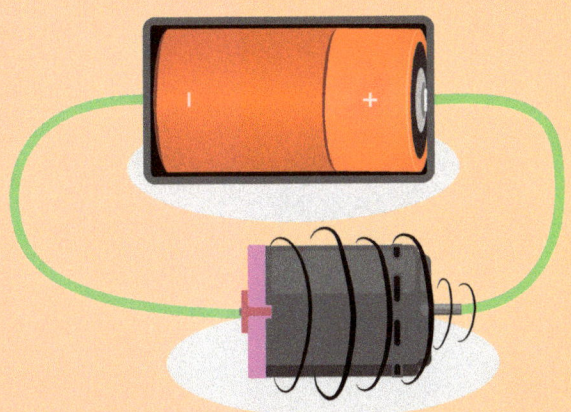

A small motor placed in a circuit would also add resistance. The electrons flowing through the motor would make it turn.

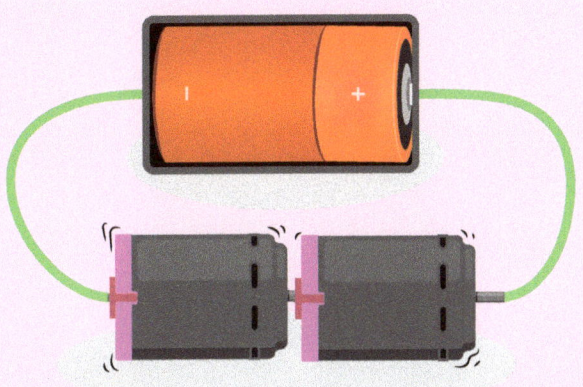

But what if you tried to put two motors in the circuit? You might get so much resistance that the electrons stop flowing and the motors won't turn at all.

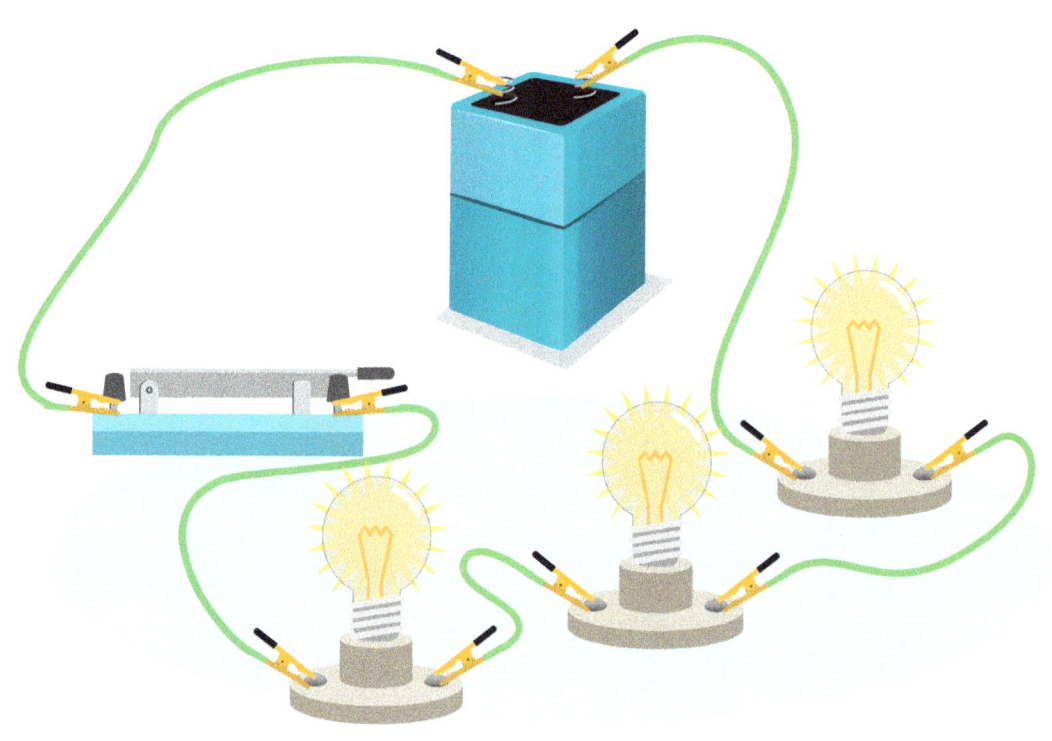

CHANGING THE RESISTANCE

For this activity you will need

- 5 alligator clip wires
- 3 6-volt mini light bulb
- 3 mini bulb sockets
- 1 knife switch
- 1 6-volt lantern battery

Steps

1. Make a circuit with a socket and bulb, a switch and a 6-volt battery. Notice how bright the bulb is.

2. Add another light bulb to the circuit. Notice what happens to the first light bulb.

3. Add a third light bulb to the circuit. Notice how bright the bulbs are now.

4. In your science journal, explain what happened when you added the light bulbs. What does this have to do with resistance?

12

There's a name for the flow of electrons in a circuit. It is called **current** (KUR int).

Just as a steady flow of water in a river is called a current, electrons flowing along a wire is also called a current.

A river can have a strong current or a weak current.

A wire can carry a strong current or a weak current.

The difference between the current in a river and a current of electrons in a wire is this:

A STRONG electrical current doesn't mean electrons are moving faster. It means there are MORE ELECTRONS that are moving through a wire.

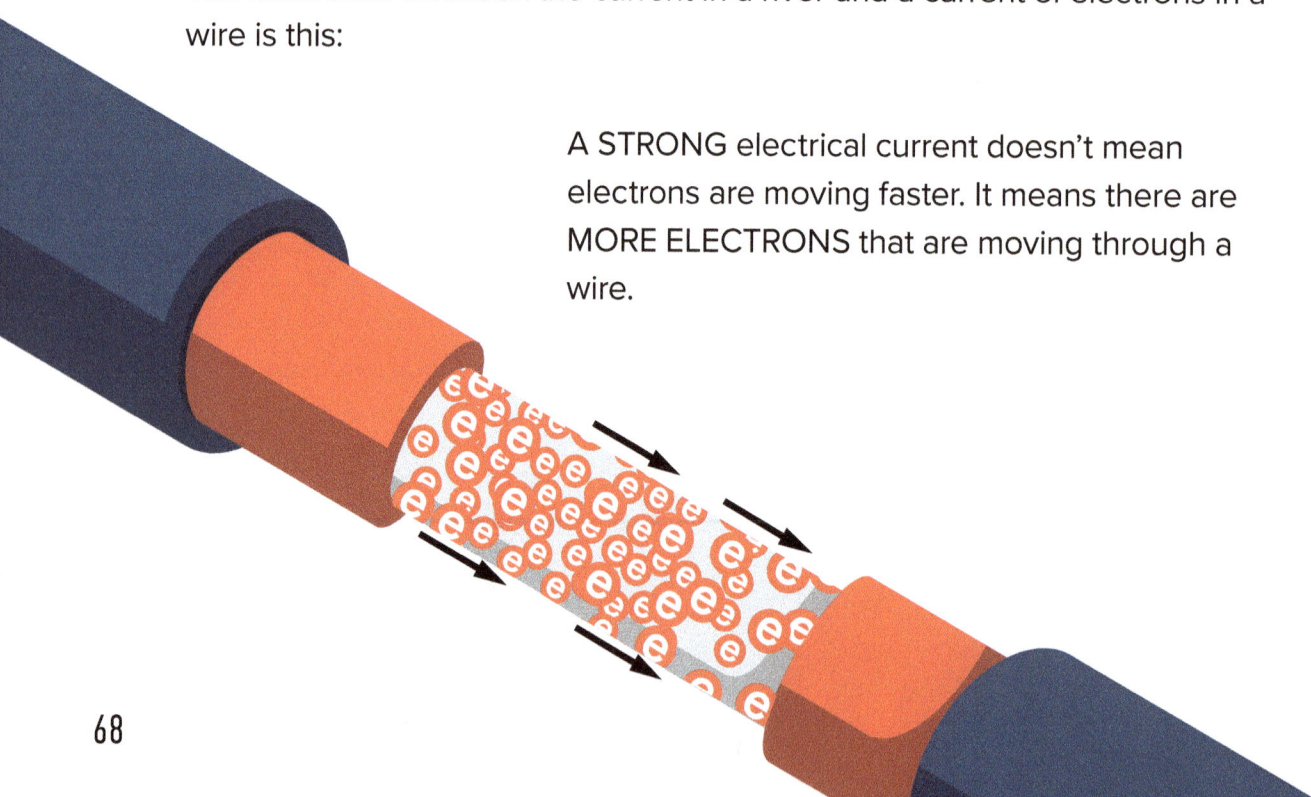

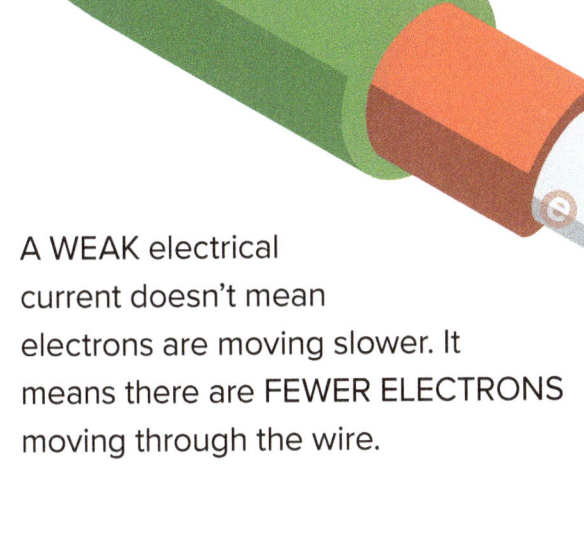

A WEAK electrical current doesn't mean electrons are moving slower. It means there are FEWER ELECTRONS moving through the wire.

We know we can't see the electrons moving in a wire because the electrons are just too small. In other words we can't see the current. But we can see how brightly a light bulb shines and this gives us a good idea how many electrons are moving through it.

A dim bulb means some electrons are moving through it. There is some current.

A brighter bulb means even more electrons are moving through it. There is more current.

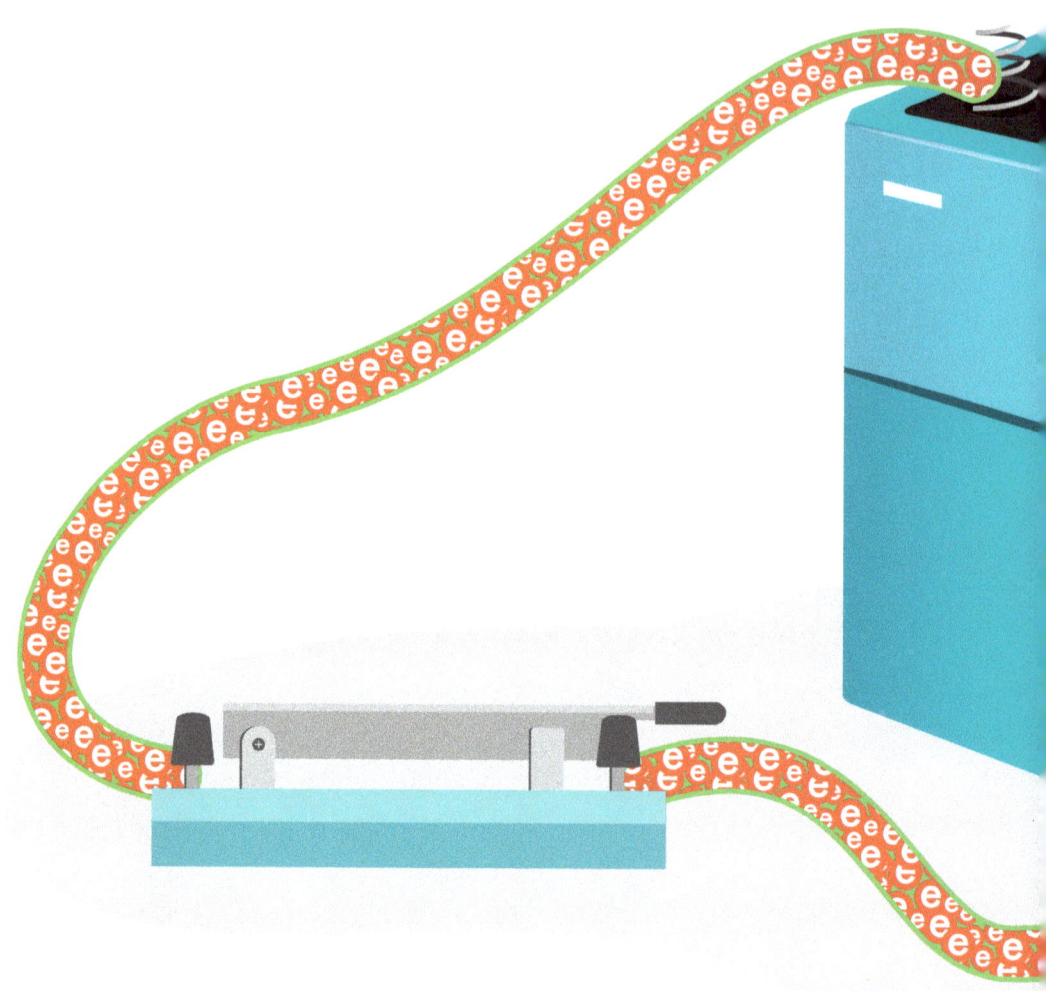

Even though electrons are jiggling very fast, they move through a circuit very slowly. In circuits like the ones you've built, it could take more than an hour for a particular electron to move all the way through the circuit.

But if you were as small as an electron, you might feel like you were moving pretty fast! Remember, there are millions and millions of atoms in the period at the end of this sentence. To move one inch, an electron moves through millions and millions of atoms!

When you close a switch, millions of stored up electrons come crowding out of the minus terminal of the battery into the wire. That forces all the electrons in the wire to be pushed forward.

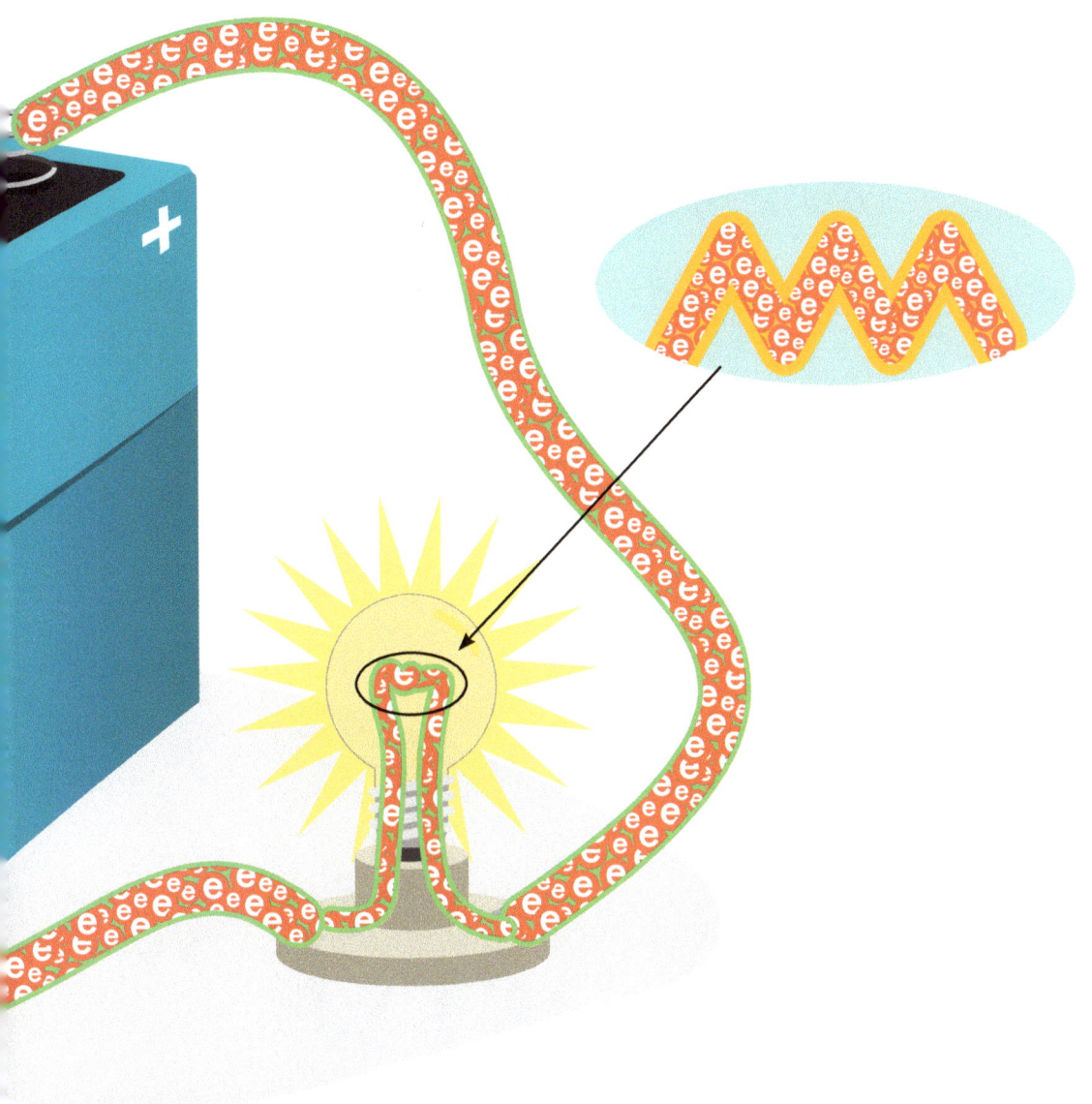

Way down the wire, electrons are crowding through the filament and are lighting the bulb. Even further down the wire, millions of electrons are crowding into the plus terminal of the battery.

None of the electrons have to move very far to make this happen.

Electrons can produce a big effect like lighting a light bulb because there are so many of them.

In fact, there are more electrons in an inch of wire than there are people on the whole planet!

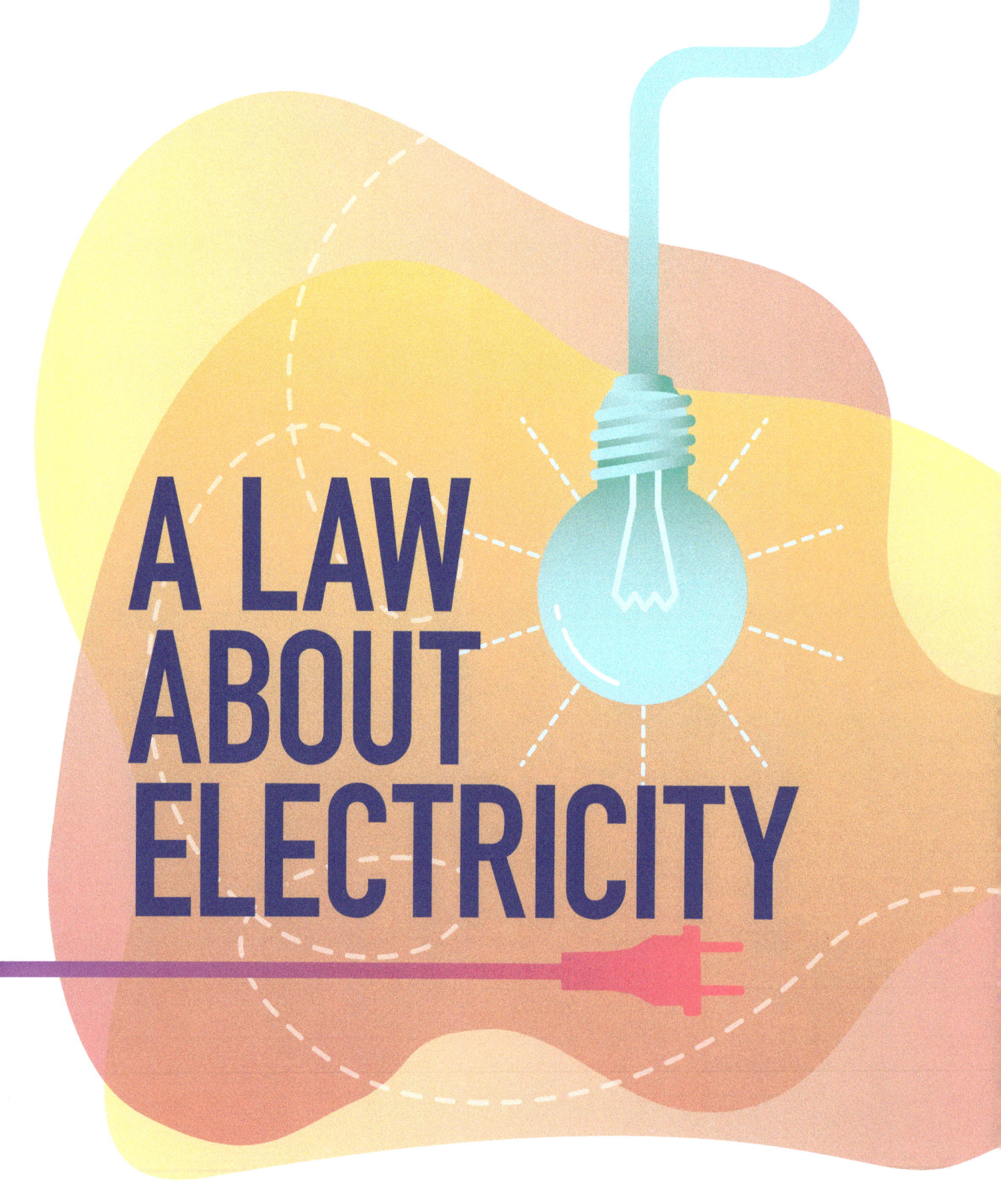

13

Earlier we learned what a scientific law is. We learned about the law of conservation of energy, which says that energy can change in form, but it will never get lost.

There is also a scientific law about electricity. And it is probably the most important law in the whole subject!

Like the words *voltage* and *volt,* this law is named after the person who first discovered it. His name was Georg Ohm, and he discovered something interesting while experimenting with Alessandro Volta's battery.

He discovered what we now call Ohm's law. It explains how voltage, current and resistance all work together.

OHM'S LAW

Let's say we have a simple circuit. There is a battery putting out some voltage and a light bulb giving some resistance.

And, of course, there is a current flowing through the wire.

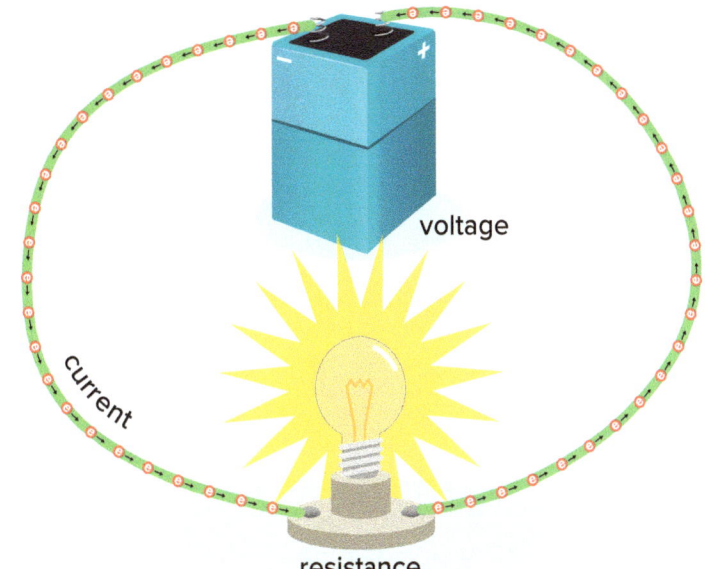

The voltage and the resistance are fighting each other over how much current can flow. The voltage is pushing the electrons forward and the resistance is pushing back, trying to slow them down.

Now, let's say we add another battery. This puts more voltage in the circuit. Two batteries can push harder than one, so you get more current. The bulb shines brighter.

Next, let's say someone comes along and starts putting more resistance in our circuit by adding more light bulbs.

With each light bulb, there is more resistance pushing back against the voltage. The result is less current. The bulbs shine dimly or not at all.

With all this resistance in the circuit, if you wanted the bulbs to shine brightly, you would have to add even more voltage.

Here is how Ohm's law works.
Let's start with two batteries and two bulbs.

More voltage makes more current.

Less voltage makes less current.

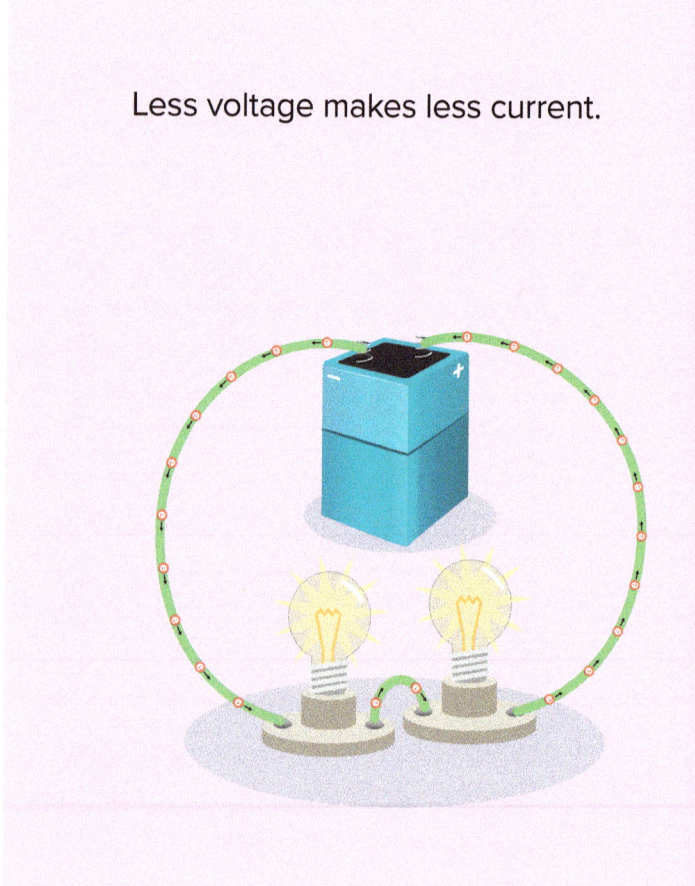

More resistance makes less current.

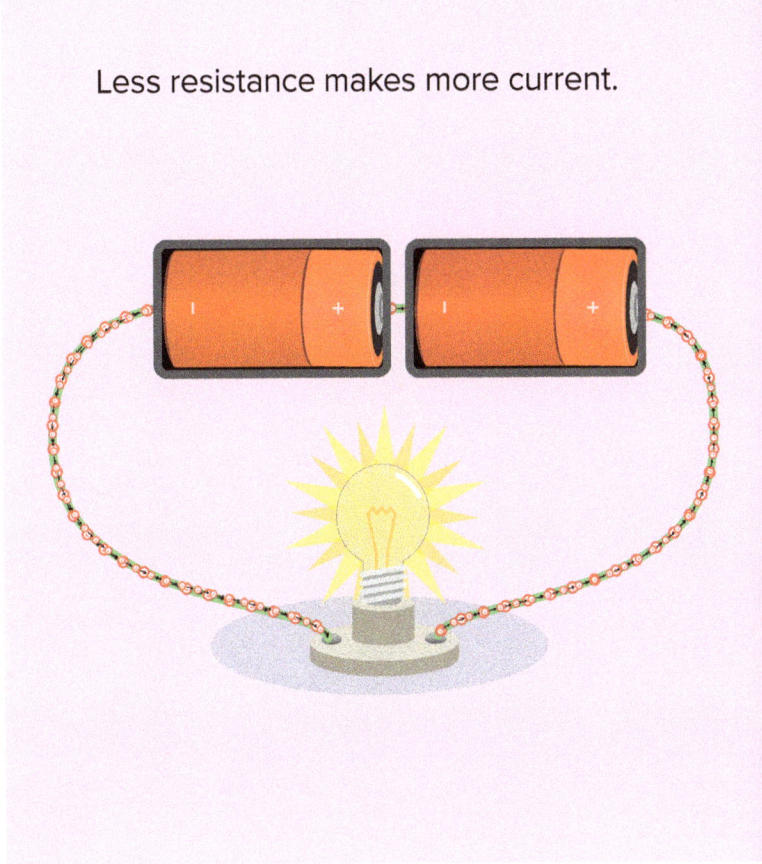

Less resistance makes more current.

Let's think of some examples of Ohm's law.

Suppose you are cooling yourself with a fan connected to a battery, but you are still hot.

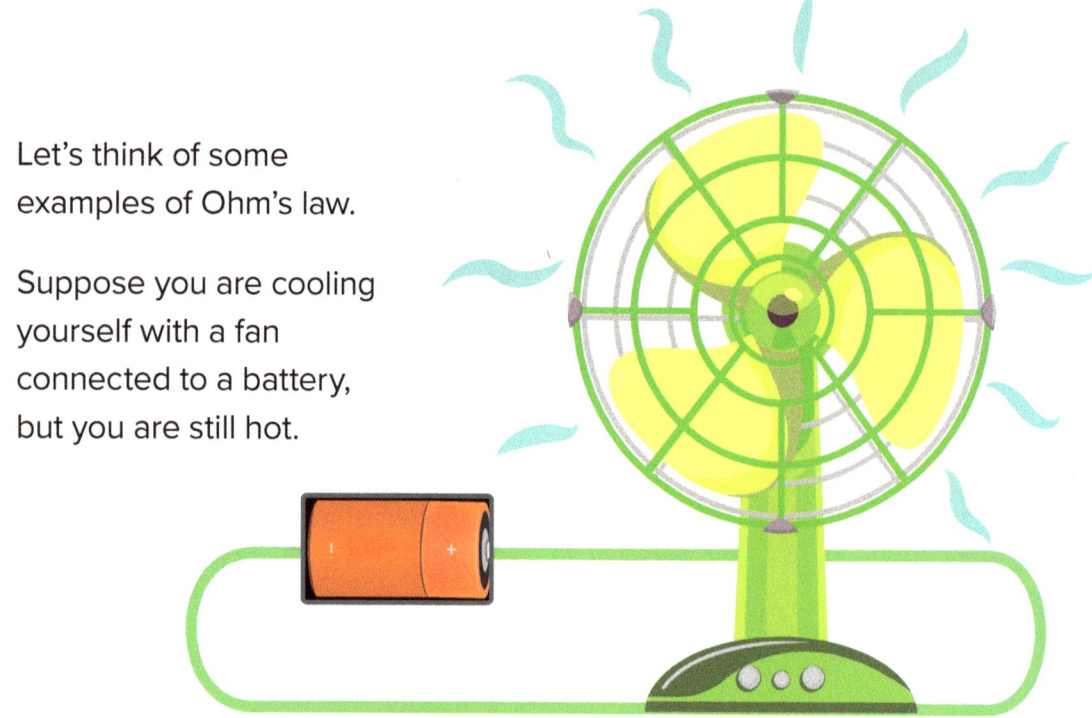

You want another fan, so you decide to add that fan to the circuit.

Ohm's law tells you that might not work well.

The voltage in the battery makes enough current flow through one fan, so it turns. The resistance of the fan isn't too much for the voltage.

But if you put another fan in the circuit, you double the resistance, while the voltage stays the same.

What happens? More resistance makes less current!

The current can't get through as well, so it goes down. Maybe it goes down so low that neither fan will run. Now instead of getting cooler you get hotter!

How do you solve this? Well, more voltage makes more current!

Two batteries will give you more voltage. Now both fans can go and you can cool yourself off better!

Here is another example of Ohm's law.

Suppose you took a flashlight that used two flashlight batteries. You want to make it brighter, so you take out the bulb and connect it to four batteries instead of two.

More voltage makes more current, right? More current will make it shine brighter.

You could try it, but the bulb might get so bright that it burns out! If it was made to work with two batteries, it might not work with four.

You could solve this by getting a bulb that was made for higher voltage. It would have a higher resistance that fit the higher voltage. And it would probably shine brighter than the two-battery bulb!

Ohm's law works for simple electrical experiments and more advanced experiments as well. Scientists use Ohm's law all the time to solve problems with electricity. And now you can too!

3V

6V

OHM'S LAW EXPERIMENT #1
MORE RESISTANCE MAKES LESS CURRENT

For this activity you will need

- 3 6-volt mini light bulbs
- 3 mini bulb sockets
- 1 knife switch
- 5 alligator clip wires
- 1 6-volt lantern battery

Steps

1. Build a circuit with one light bulb, a 6-volt battery and a switch. Notice the brightness of the bulb.

2. Connect two light bulbs to the battery and switch. Notice the brightness of the bulbs.

3. Connect three light bulbs to the battery and switch. Notice the brightness of the bulbs.

4. What did you see happen? In your science journal, tell how Ohm's law explains what happened.

OHM'S LAW EXPERIMENT #2
MORE VOLTAGE MAKES MORE CURRENT

For this activity you will need

- 3 6-volt mini mini bulbs
- 3 mini bulb sockets
- 1 knife switch
- 7 alligator clip wires
- 3 6-volt lantern batteries

Steps

1. Build a circuit with three light bulbs, two six-volt batteries and a switch. Notice the brightness of the bulbs.

2. Connect another 6-volt battery to make three batteries and three light bulbs. Notice the brightness of the bulbs.

3. What did you see happen? In your science journal, tell how Ohm's law explains what happened.

OHM'S LAW EXPERIMENT #3
USING OHM'S LAW TO RUN A MOTOR

For this activity you will need

- 1 6-volt mini light bulb
- 1 mini bulb socket
- 1 knife switch
- 8 alligator clip wires
- 4 1.5-volt D-cell batteries
- 4 D-cell battery holders
- 2 6-volt lantern batteries
- 1 12-volt DC mini-motor

Steps

1. Make a circuit with the motor, 2 6-volt batteries, and a switch. Notice how fast the motor runs.

2. Now put a small light bulb in the circuit also. Notice how fast the motor runs.

3. Add batteries to the circuit one at a time until the motor is running as fast (or almost as fast) as it did at the beginning. Be sure you don't run it too long. You don't want your batteries to go dead! Also don't make the motor run faster than it did in step 1 or you might burn out the motor.

4. What did you see happen? In your science journal, tell how Ohm's law explains what happened.

14

Now that you know something about electricity, and you've built different circuits and demonstrated Ohm's law at work, you can explore and find out even more.

There are so many directions you can go!

Where does the electricity in your house come from? How does it get there?

Why do you get a shock when you touch a doorknob?

What about solar energy? What does electricity have to do with that?

How do we get electricity from the wind?

What are some exciting new ways scientists are finding to produce electricity?

If you're interested in any of these questions, or other questions of your own, the answers are out there just waiting for you.

After all, you're a young scientist.
Go find out!

www.ingramcontent.com/pod-product-compliance
Lightning Source LLC
Chambersburg PA
CBHW040312240426
43666CB00026B/2936